# FAILURE, INC.

# FAILURE, INC.

## 52 WAYS TO GO UNDER IN BUSINESS

## HOWARD EISNER

Capital Ideas for Business and Personal Development

CAPITAL
BOOKS, INC.
Sterling, Virginia

Capital Books, Inc.
P.O. Box 605
Herndon, Virginia 20172-0605

ISBN 13: 978-1-933102-40-5

**Library of Congress Cataloging-in-Publication Data**
Eisner, Howard, 1935-
   Failure, Inc. : 52 ways to go under in business / Howard
Eisner.
      p. cm. — (Capital ideas for business & personal
development series)
   ISBN 978-1-933102-40-5 (alk. paper)
   1. Success in business. 2. Business failures. I. Title. II.
Series.

   HF5386.E35 2007
   658.1'6—dc22

                                    2007013144

Printed in the United States of America on acid-free paper
that meets the American National Standards Institute Z39-
48 Standard.

First Edition

10 9 8 7 6 5 4 3 2 1

*I dedicate this book to my wife, June Linowitz.*

Without her support, this book would likely not have progressed beyond a set of ideas to a reality of written text. Her intuition about management behavior is something very special. She is also a master at multi-tasking and "getting it done." I've learned many lessons from just listening to her, and watching her solve problems. At times, I've been a participant in her "process." I look forward to more of the same as we travel down the road together.

# ACKNOWLEDGMENTS

I would like, first, to acknowledge the support, insight, and professionalism of my publisher, Kathleen Hughes. It has been a pleasure to work with her on this book. It reminds me of a last line in the movie *Casablanca*, in which Humphrey Bogart and Claude Rains are leaving the airport and one of them says, "This could be the beginning of an excellent relationship," or something like it. So, to Kathleen I say: This could be the beginning of a book writing and publishing adventure together.

I also wish to acknowledge the indirect contributions of:

▶ People who are aware of their mistakes and who learn from them

▶ Companies that have embraced "continuous improvement" in one way or another  (Paths to long term success are usually taken one step at a time, and with due regard for how to change course when it is necessary to do so.)

▶ Companies cited here that have done something special or noteworthy

▶ Specific people cited here who have done something special to advance the state-of-the-art in management theory or practice, or in both

▶ My thoughtful students who are able to question conventional wisdom and take their appropriate places in industry, government and academia.

# CONTENTS

# INTRODUCTION

As the title says, this is a book about how to fail in business. Why would you be interested in prescriptions for failure? After all, wouldn't it make more sense if I wrote about how to succeed? Strangely, the answer to that last question is "NO." There are many books about how to succeed, and (a) people are tired of the same old boring suggestions, and (b) few can claim great success by having followed the suggestions contained in them.

So this book tries a different tack, based upon the proposition that fear of failure makes a more direct and lasting impression. For some reason, people pay a lot more attention to "ways to fail" than they do to "ways to succeed." I've tried this numerous times with my university graduate students. They are shocked to discover that their organization is already quite a way down the road on about a half dozen ways to fail. At that point the realization sets in as they say: "I'm already failing and I didn't even know it!" Another often heard reaction is: "My boss is already doing all these things. I knew he was leading us down the road to failure!" In the former case, where students have immediate control over their company's actions, they vow to turn things around as soon as they get back to the office. If they are not in charge, the common reaction is anger, and even a determination to ditch the boss and move on to a completely different scenario. Why be caught up with a bad boss and get painted by the broad brush of failure? A third reaction is to blame a department head or a VP who seems to be determined to fail. In just about all these situations, being part of failure appears to bring with it a greater sense of urgency. "Let's not be part of this; let's do something else and do it now!"

The psychology of failure is a strange thing. Most people do not believe they are failing, at least overtly, in the world of business. It's hard to come to terms with it, even if the news is coming from your immediate manager. "There's something wrong here, but it's not with me. My boss doesn't understand my value, or how to use me." Wherever the fault lies, there are a whole lot of disconnects out there. Are you one of the folks who are in denial, one way or another?

If so, I hope the 52 ways to fail offered here, one for each week of the year, will help you get out of it—before it's too late. You've got seven days to ruminate about each one, and a full year to think about the lot of them. And if you get off just one train that's on a track to failure, it will be worth many times the modest price of this short book. Good luck to all in your search for ways to get back on track.

# AFTER LABORING OVER YOUR STRATEGIC PLAN, IGNORE IT FOR A YEAR

Why is this a strategy for failure? At best, you've just wasted your own and your executives' valuable time. At worst, you'll miss opportunities for positive change and new directions for your organization every month of the year.

Developing a strategic plan takes the key players in a company at least a month of intense work. Many are newly energized by the goals of the plan—envisioning new worlds to conquer and uplifting times in the process. The number of new initiatives is a variable, perhaps ranging from five to ten, especially if you are talking about relatively minor adjustments to an "old" initiative. The concepts, of course, are strategic in nature, rather than focusing on tactical details. Here's where many managers have a chance to shine by converting the strategies to operational tactics. For many, what could be more fun?

Managers return to their offices with the newly hatched strategic plan under their belts. Often they are quite excited about what the plan says and what it implies in terms of new challenges for the coming year. They are ready to pass along the strategic goals the plan embodies, such as the following:

▶ Opening up a new "line of business" (LOB)

- ▶ Challenging your most serious competitor
- ▶ Upgrading old legacy information systems
- ▶ Reengineering certain business processes
- ▶ Starting new employee training and education programs
- ▶ Beginning a modest acquisition program.

These and other agreed-upon actions should help to energize the entire company. Managers will find new levels of positive actions that can be devoted to their jobs and to the company. They will share their excitement with their people as soon as they return from the planning sessions. What could go wrong at this point? Apparently, a lot.

If you file the plan away for a year, you are implying that it does not guide or relate to monthly actions in any significant way. That, of course, is a serious mistake.

A natural point of connection is the "monthly measurement" meeting, where the company measures its progress toward agreed-upon goals. Strategic goals, or related tactical matters, should be a part of this process. In this particular way, it is possible to breathe life into the strategic plan each month, and thereby try to make sure that its final resting place is not the ubiquitous circular file. On the other hand, you can begin your journey toward failure with this first item on our list, and make sure that your best strategic thinking does not see the light of day for eleven of the twelve months of the year.

# Hire Smart Folks, Then Don't Listen to Them

Many companies know it's important to hire the very best people they can find. So they go to extraordinary lengths to find such people, "wining and dining" them until the recruit says yes. Then, for some inexplicable reason, benign neglect sets in. All the "hiring" words are forgotten along with the progressive actions that the candidate seemed to make possible during the hiring discussions. The bureaucracy asserts itself from the first day of employment forward.

Of course, this makes no sense at all. And much of the responsibility for selecting this mode of failure lies with the new hire's immediate boss. Yes, you're the culprit, even though you might want to blame it on someone else, like the VPs or "company policy." The care and feeding of your new hire is *your* responsibility for sure, and needs to be carried out with dedication and forethought. What is the new hire's immediate assignment as well as long-term vista? How can communication channels be established and maintained? How can your new hire be part of your established and functional high performance team? How can you tap into his or her new ideas?

There are many cases that demonstrate how companies hire extraordinary people and then proceed to pay almost no attention to them. The classic, if you will, is the matter of Xerox PARC (Palo Alto Research Center). Xerox, having established itself as one of the new technology firms to contend with, decided to set up an R&D center far away from corporate machinations in the eastern part of the country. They hired excellent people and set them in motion. Budgets for explorations of new technologies were not a problem. As it turned out, new and wonderful results were indeed forthcoming in such areas as:[1]

- ▶ Computer architectures
- ▶ Software languages
- ▶ Input devices (e.g., mouse)
- ▶ Connectivity (e.g., networks)
- ▶ Human machine interfaces.

However, when it came to bringing these results to the market, the company backed up several steps, apparently not wanting to take new risks of that type. So the people got frustrated and went off to seek their fortunes elsewhere. And Xerox was not able to make use of all the new ground that had been plowed. In the aggregate, it is possible that they did not take advantage of billions of dollars of new technologies that later showed their commercial value.

A clear way to fail is not to properly value each and every new employee, and not to understand how to obtain the very best from his or her efforts. Each new hire is a fresh opportunity to create something new and exciting, for today and tomorrow.

---

[1] Robert X. Cringely, *Accidental Empires* (Addison Wesley, 1992).

# 3
# SPEND YOUR WHOLE BUDGET ON BUILDING YOUR PRODUCT— IT WILL SELL ITSELF

If you're not Campbell's and you make and sell soup, you know it takes more than a superior product to have a successful business. Too many other folks make and sell soup, and of course they compete head-to-head with you. To have a chance at success, people need to find out about your product and take the risk of buying it. Are there any counterexamples? Let's try taking a brief look at:

1. Microsoft
2. Netscape, and
3. Google

At first glance, one might conclude that these three "products" sold themselves. In the case of MS DOS, Microsoft developed the product "on top of" another operating system (Q-DOS) and to the specifications of their customer, IBM. This wonderful deal for Microsoft proceeded in a "piggyback" mode. For every IBM PC sold, the operating system went along for the ride. And IBM put its full marketing power behind the sale of its new line of small computers. It doesn't get any better than that.

Netscape and Google, one might argue, are examples of the notion that marketing is not necessarily required.

"Word of mouth" was a powerful force that gave birth to the widespread use of these extraordinary products. But then, where is Netscape today? It was bought by AOL, then merged into Time-Warner. Google is a giant today. But Netscape and Google are only a couple of cases in a field of perhaps millions of products. Word of mouth marketing is usually not a viable strategy. The odds are too long against success.

The path to a sustainable product is usually long and arduous. One helpful device along the road, especially proven with software, is the User's Group. Holding conferences of User Groups supports the product with lots of information as well as lots of dollars. I've seen literally decades of SAS User Group meetings, with happy participants and faithful users.

If we move away from software, we see dramatic examples of companies clearly spending fortunes to get word of their products into the hands of old and new customers. Perhaps the most noticeable of these come from the automotive industry. There we see, in commercials, extraordinary products such as cars that increase their speed to a point where they begin to soar into the sky. Someone authorized that commercial and spent a boatload of money on it. So much for products that can "sell themselves."

So, there are two ways to go. Believe that your product will sell itself, which is more-or-less the equivalent of winning the lottery. The longer range path to potential success is just to spend the money for an orchestrated marketing campaign to launch your product. You need a "smart" approach as to "how" to advertise your product. For more about this, see suggestion number nine, and pick up a few books on the fine art of product advertising and branding.

# THE BEST TRAINING FOR YOUR NEW PROJECT MANAGERS IS ON THE JOB

Why would you come to this conclusion? There are actually several possible reasons, none of them irrational.

The first might be because you became a serious Project Manager yourself without any formal PM training. That's quite powerful since we tend to believe that if "it worked for me it must therefore work for others." Another reason might be that you've seen several PM training courses and have concluded that none of them was worth anything: too much expense, not enough real world application. Again, an argument not to be taken lightly. Yet a third reason is simply that you believe that on-the-job training (OJT) is the right way to go in terms of results and expenses. You've seen it work, and very well at that, including with you.

So, does no formal PM training work? Answer: It might. However, that's not good enough. A "hit and miss" proposition is just simply not sufficient, especially when you're looking at this very important PM position. The "miss" part can lead to poor results for lots of people, as well as the overall enterprise. The "miss" part can lead to horror stories of various shapes and sizes. Here's a list of ten typical mistakes that the untrained PM may be especially prone to, with each mistake potentially leading to a significant problem for the enterprise:

1. No coherent and effective "project plan"
2. No special contingency plans for different types of contracts (e.g., fixed price vs. cost reimbursable, etc.)
3. No building of teams
4. No formal risk analysis and mitigation activities
5. Inferior technical approach to project requirements
6. Poor "people" relationships with members of the project team
7. Poor interactions with the boss (of the PM)
8. Project not completed according to the agreed-upon schedule
9. Overspending so as to "blow the project budget"
10. Alienation and permanent loss of customer.

If the above errors can each lead to quite serious consequences, the organization absolutely *must* find ways to keep this from occurring. To do otherwise is to be unaware of the responsibilities of the enterprise. Assumptions about how people learn and what OJT has provided are not good enough. We must be able to verify that the PMs have the requisite skill sets to perform somewhere between "good" and "excellent."

Even though a PM position may be considered an entry point into management, the level of project responsibilities may be quite high, as measured by such aspects as key customer satisfaction, likelihood of follow-on business, profitability, as well as others. Serious and well thought out PM training is, therefore, more than highly recommended. It can be critical and should be an integral part of company policy. Failure to do so can put one foot on that slippery slope and one foot on a banana peel.

# SHIFT EXCLUSIVELY TO GROWTH BY ACQUISITION WHEN YOUR ORGANIC GROWTH BOGS DOWN

The key word here is "exclusively." It implies that you have given up on organic growth and are now on the path of acquisitions as your *only* approach.

This reminds me of a person with a temporarily injured leg trying to move around by hopping on the good leg. He or she may be able to get from A to B, but not very well and not without some increased risk. And covering up the injured leg with layers of clothing doesn't really hide the problem either.

Many companies and people have embraced quite aggressive acquisition programs. A few come easily to mind, such as Jim Ling (of LTV fame), Norman Augustine (ex-president of Lockheed Martin), Harold Geneen (of ITT) and Bernard Schwartz (of Loral). Each had acquisitions as a centerpiece for growth; but quite serious efforts, in all cases, were put into internal growth and how to achieve it. In short, acquisitions were not the only aspect of growing a healthy and successful company.

During the course of my thirty years in industry, my company (a) sold itself twice, (b) bought itself back (from a parent company) once, (c) acquired two completely separate companies (after the acquisition of one of them, I became its president).

9

Acquiring a company is a very serious and non-trivial adventure. Here are some of the parts of that adventure that need to be addressed (and worried about) in some detail:

1.  How to achieve a sense of balance in the "benefits packages" (not necessarily complete equity among them)
2.  How to assure that both companies continue to see and experience the benefits of the acquisition
3.  How to create new opportunities for the key people in both companies
4.  How to re-align the corporate cultures in the best possible way
5.  How to keep the two companies from stepping on each others' toes
6.  How to continuously improve cash flow and profitability
7.  How to achieve the often elusive efficiencies and synergies
8.  How to treat both companies fairly (objectively and by perception).

Doing all of the above correctly is hard, not easy. Each has its own formula for how to get bogged down, and how to fail.

On the side of recovering one's ability to grow internally, that too is a difficult question—but one that must be addressed. Unfortunately, there is no one formula since the answers depend a great deal on how and why the organic growth got bogged down in the first place. Get your best managers and thinkers in a room and put the question to them. It may take a while, but a roadmap for a new and energized growth plan will eventually emerge. Trust yourself and trust your people to find the problem(s) as well as the solution(s). If, for some reason, you don't want to do that, you have probably added another dimension to Failure, Incorporated.

# MEETINGS TAKE KEY MANAGERS AWAY FROM THEIR REAL WORK

This approach may be selected by those who (a) are basically antisocial, (b) do not wish to be challenged by subordinates in an open meeting, (c) believe that e-mail has made the face-to-face meeting obsolete, (d) like to operate in a "command and control" style, and/or (e) various combinations of the above. This approach may also be a concrete sign of the fear of losing control, and perhaps a basic feeling of inadequacy in group situations.

Meetings are, indeed, very important to the lifeblood of an organization. Meetings may be short or long, periodic or on-demand, timed or open-ended, but they can represent a very positive way to do the following:

1.  Spread the culture you desire
2.  Identify problem areas worthy of solution
3.  Solve problems
4.  Show subordinates how to manage (i.e., train your people)
5.  Resolve conflict
6.  Listen for alternative views/opinions
7.  Encourage teamwork and team building
8.  Observe the actions of your people
9.  Figure out how to beat your competition
10. Build trust and participative management.

Notwithstanding the above, poorly planned meetings use people's time unwisely. Some of that evidence comes from one of our most serious management gurus, Peter Drucker. In a quite early book,[1] Drucker comments that "the manner in which an executive does productive work may still be a major waste of somebody else's time." In a treatise from another author ten years later, but all about Drucker,[2] he remains consistent in this arena: "The manager should not be cavalier about wasting the time of others." There is little question that Drucker, over the years, was a champion of the people. He was quite protective of their time, and required the boss to be seriously disciplined in this regard.

Having said that, we need to acknowledge the role that meetings played in Harold Geneen's wildly successful career at ITT.[3] Geneen held meeting after meeting with large numbers of his people for just about all of his eighteen year presidency. He points out that normal general manager meetings ran from ten in the morning to ten at night. At times, a meeting would continue on beyond that until Geneen felt that the topic at hand had been fully explored. He was looking for open, free, face-to-face communications and believed that large-scale meetings were the primary way to achieve that. Hard to argue with, considering his record.

[1] Peter Drucker, *The Effective Executive* (Harper & Row, 1966).
[2] J. Tarrant, *Drucker* (Warner Books, 1976).
[3] Harold Geneen, with A. Moscow, *Managing* (Avon Books, 1984).

# SENIOR PEOPLE DON'T REQUIRE PROGRESS CHECKS

Senior people often believe they do not require any guidance or discussion. This is a distinct weakness and encourages too much independence and possible loss of company wide goals. Too much time off by oneself may lead to going too far down the wrong road. This, in turn, may lead to various types of disasters, like making "lost leader" deals with customers.

Having many senior people reporting to you is indeed a blessing. But "senior" does not automatically mean "error-free." We all eventually make errors—even you, dear reader. And we can minimize these errors and their effects by some relatively simple tracking ideas and actions. Indeed, perhaps the simplest was articulated by Peters and Waterman in their landmark book, *In Search of Excellence*.[1] They called it MBWA, Management By Walking Around. You bet! It's all about showing your interest and staying in touch. It's all about being involved. It's all about ensuring progress, or otherwise.

Suppose you have ten projects reporting to ten PMs who are all senior people reporting to you, Ms. Vice Presi-

[1] T. Peters and R. Waterman, Jr., *In Search of Excellence* (Harper & Row, 1982).

dent. Now go back and take a hard look at the various mistakes these PMs can be making. Mucho opportunities to fail. Enough to make your head spin. Do you simply assume that since they are all senior, they'll come to you if they have a problem? Or do you need a tad more involvement (control) through some more specific actions?

Quite a few years back I hired a vice president for my company, under the usual wide-ranging freedom to act embedded in the small print of the plans and procedures manual. My company had evolved a serious "authority matrix" that helped to define boundaries, even at the VP level. Then one day, this VP conceived of a "deal" for a customer and proceeded to "sell it" to that customer. It was a sweetheart deal for the customer, but a bad one for the company. When I found out about it, happily before we signed a contract with that customer, I knew I had some fixing to do. I met immediately with my VP and went "through the math" with him, in considerable detail. His inexperience in this particular market led him down the wrong road, which he acknowledged. We then both went to see the customer to revise the "deal." It was, as I recall, a very difficult conversation. However, the customer ultimately appreciated our honesty and reasons, as well as the prominence of our tails between our legs. He accepted our revised deal that was now a good thing for both his company and our company. It was a win-win solution instead of a "they win–we lose" proposition. Thank goodness for customers like that and my luck at being able to intercede before a contract was signed.

You can't button up everything, even with a well-documented authority matrix (who can do what, when, and where). This interaction between company president (me) and new vice president (him) helped to convince me that MBWA had some real and tangible merit. And I also decided that monthly measurements needed more teeth, along with ways to shorten the tether.

# PEOPLE DON'T LIKE BAD NEWS, SO NEVER REPORT ANY

Everything they said was positive and uplifting. The company was doing extremely well. Beating projections. Record this and record that. Wall Street would be happy. The stock price would certainly go up. And then the truth came out, and everyone noticed the difference between the announcements and the realities. And then the stock price took a dive; and with it, lots of stock options went "under water." And the level of trust between the workers and management continued to erode. That can often be the beginning of the end.

No, it doesn't have to be the size and shape of ENRON. Over time, little "lies" and "spin" will cause people to lose faith in a company. And once they do, if they are able to, they will (a) look for another job (if they're inside the company), and (b) look for another investment (if they're outside the company).

David Packard, one of the two founders of HP, explains that a cornerstone of "The HP Way"[1] is building a deep and abiding "trust in people." Lies and spin are antithetical to trust, so what is required is an unswerving dedication to truth. Pushing the truth around will invariably

---

[1] D. Packard, *The HP Way* (HarperCollins, 1995).

get you and the company into big trouble. In HP's case, even the recent indiscretion at the top cannot really destroy the company's many years of "straight shooting."

Another aspect of this attitude, at a local level, is that people inside the company who want to help cannot do so since the boss won't acknowledge that there is a problem. A boss who conveys the truth is more likely to have people step up to challenging problem-solving tasks. What could be better than that? But it starts with honesty rather than obfuscation.

So what do some other practitioners tell us about how to deal with a person who is an unhealthy mix between Polyanna and a Madison Avenue "spinner?" A person who is not completely devoted to honesty would likely not last more than five minutes at Harold Geneen's ITT. In his own words,[2] Geneen insisted upon "open, free, and honest communications up and down the ranks of our management structure." Even if you had bad news, at his landmark meetings, it was time to tell the truth, 100 percent. And Norman Augustine, ex-chairman of Lockheed Martin, focused on trust (among other good things) to allow an enterprise to get through a crisis.[3] Building trust was one consequence of their Ethics Hot Line, as they insisted upon ethical behavior in every nook and cranny of the company.

And the bottom line? If you're the boss, talk the truth, even if it casts negatively on the company performance and situation. Display competence by revealing what you and the company have decided is the appropriate way to fix the problem(s). Show confidence that despite a possible setback, there is no question that the company will overcome all difficulties, large and small. Be a leader, not a wimp!

---

[2] H. Geneen, with A. Moscow, *Managing* (Avon Books, 1984).
[3] N. Augustine, *Augustine's Travels* (AMACOM, 1998).

# Spend Your Whole Budget on Marketing—Making the Product Is Easy

This is basically the opposite of Failure Technique 3, leading to the conclusion that either extreme in spending—for marketing or product development—is likely to move you in the direction of failure. A few reasons why this particular extreme can be harmful are the following:

1.  You can't get the product built without spending
2.  The product developers feel de-valued and frustrated, and
3.  They quit, leading to the conclusion that you will have essentially no current *or* future products, meaning that
4.  True failure is right around the corner, and soon to be fully realized.

Once again, we have incorporated failure into our corporate plans—in this case into our budget allocation process.

It has been noted, from time to time, that marketing folks have a built-in bias toward marketing as the most vital of all business activities. To them, if you can't market a product, even from a picture and spec sheet, there's something wrong with the product, so go back and re-do it, and they'll then try again.

Another scenario is that a marketer and a customer are talking. The customer says she could buy the product if it had some new specific features. The marketer says, "We can do that, just sign here." Signature in hand, it's back to the office, insisting that the features be added by tomorrow. Chalk up another marketing success, and a good reason to hire another marketing person.

Of course, no company (hopefully) would literally spend its *whole* budget on marketing and completely starve the product development folks. Given that perspective, the next question might be: What is the proper balance of marketing expenditures to product development expenditures? The answer is that there is no one answer since there are a whole lot of variables that need to be taken into account, on both sides of the equation. But please keep the following in mind as you search for an answer:

1.   If you don't have a product that you can *demonstrate*, you are not likely to be able to sell it;
2.   If you can demonstrate your product, but not to enough potential customers, you are not likely to generate sufficient sales;
3.   If your sales revenues are too low, you may have to reduce costs, which could mean reduced budgets for *both* marketing and sales;
4.   Under (3) above, a downward spiral might then ensue, resulting in an increased probability of failure.

As we have said, there are, indeed, lots of pathways to backward motion in Failure, Inc.

# IF THE PROCESS IS RIGHT, THE RESULTING PRODUCT WILL BE RIGHT

There is no question that having the correct process is an important aspect of getting the product right. However, it is not the *only* factor; and so we must be careful about applying this "principle" across the board.

If we are producing "widgets" of one sort or another, then we may well expect close to 100 percent adherence to this principle. For example, if you are making toys in a totally automated process, the products should be identical and correct, unless there are equipment failures. With no human intervention, and with appropriate design and its verification, proper process more-or-less guarantees proper product. So why then is this on our list of possible ways to fail?

The basic problem arises when the human element is an integral part of the process. Further, the role of the human can be quite variable, as in the difference between a simple assembly line task, and one in which considerable judgment is exercised as in developing software for a system. And the latter gives us an area that has been prominent in the discussion of process and product.

Some years ago, under the sponsorship of the Department of Defense, the Software Engineering Institute (SEI) of Carnegie Mellon University defined a Capability Maturity Model (CMM) that measured the degree to which an organization was capable of developing acceptable software. This basic notion has since been expanded to an *integrated* CMM (the CMMI), focused on the key process areas that need to be mastered in order to have both good software and good systems. Implicit in all of this was the notion that if you get the process (areas) right, there would be a high likelihood that the product would also be right. This notion has more-or-less been widely accepted. It is accepted in this book as well. The problem with blanket acceptance is largely embedded in the human element. Here is an example.

Suppose an organization knows exactly how to carry out all elements of the CMM. But due to a lack of software engineers, they assign a group of nuclear engineers to develop software for their next important project. Although the nuclear engineers may be very smart and very talented, there is little chance they will develop good software, no matter how well they have been trained in the CMM processes.

In short, a good process is a necessary condition for the right product, but it is insufficient. You also need specific and comprehensive subject matter expertise to ensure the correct product. One might say that if you have both the right process as well as the right subject matter expertise, you will have a very high likelihood that the product will be what you want it to be, i.e., right process + right subject expertise = right product. And we will take another look at "process" when we have a chance to explore Business Process Reengineering (BPR) (see chapter 49).

# Don't Worry about Industry Trends—Your Company Is the Trendsetter

There are, indeed, lots of companies that are trendsetters: IBM, Microsoft, Apple, Google, and Disney. Should they decide not to worry about trends? No way. Consider this story.

In 1988, a multi-billion dollar technology enterprise was, without doubt, at the very top of their industry. They were producing unique sets of both hardware and software, and were acknowledged market leaders. But some four years later, they filed for bankruptcy. What a shock. A clearly astonishing piece of news in the industry. The name of that company was Wang Laboratories.

Wang was the leader in word processing systems, in both their hardware and their software. On just about every secretary's desk were Wang word processors, and the company was flying high. We do not know how they approached the issue of trendsetting, but there is no doubt that they missed a trend or two and that led to their demise. One trend had to do with a shift toward "open" personal computer (PC) systems, also called "clones," so that consumers no longer needed Wang proprietary computers. In conjunction with this trend was the fact that specialty software houses were producing word processing software (like Wordstar, Multimate, and others) that could be run on these PC systems. No need to have to go to Wang;

excellent alternatives were now available. This basically pulled the rug out from under Wang, and set the industry on a different course. Good for the consumer; bad for Wang Labs.

There are other examples that prove that failure to observe trends, even though you're a market leader, can lead to disaster. Both Xerox and IBM failed to see the trends accurately. In the case of Xerox, they set up Xerox PARC (Palo Alto Research Center) and then failed to listen to what PARC was saying and producing. With IBM, they clearly failed to see the true value of software, even though they were market leaders, and let Microsoft wind up the winner.

Companies, even market leaders, must be tracking trends on a regular basis. Microsoft does this in a most serious way, understanding that IBM's early failure gave them the foothold they needed to be one of the most successful companies of our time. However, they missed the Google success when it was right there in front of them to pursue. Who would have expected that a search engine could be that valuable?

Back in the seventies, the company I was with came to be a sister company to an enterprise called Yankelovich, Skelly and White, better known as YSW. During my many conversations with them, especially White, it became clear how valuable trend information could be. Looking at one of their "products," the Yankelovich "Monitor," I could see that market trend information was vital and that many market leaders subscribed to that information. Trends were published in the "Monitor" product that explored, with survey-based numbers, such areas as introspection, creativity, and change. We can assume that the success of this type of information product indicates that lots of folks *were* paying attention, and that missteps were likely avoided as one kept track of what people were thinking about, and purchasing. To fail to do so, even as a trendsetter, might contribute to your own downward trend. Even the mighty Ford Motor Company is trying to figure out what they did wrong, what they missed, and when they missed it.

# SPEND LOTS OF MONEY ON R&D, BUT DON'T PAY ATTENTION TO THE RESULTS

Why would an organization spend a bundle on research and development (R&D), but not wait for the results? It often happens with action-oriented folks of the "don't-bother-me-with-facts-my-mind-is-already-made-up" type. It can also happen as a result of a bureaucratic struggle between two vice presidents—one in charge of R&D, and the other(s) in a different "line" part of the organization. The R&D VP has his or her say, and so does the other VP. Then there is a kind of arm-wrestle, leading, unfortunately, to a win-lose conclusion. The line VP wins, and the R&D VP loses. This is not a far-fetched scenario.

Consider the "poster-child" for this sort of behavior: Xerox Corporation and its famous Palo Alto Research Center (PARC). In 1970 Xerox put big-time money into this research facility. Recognizing that the xerographic process they had invested in was the key to their success, it made sense to make another major investment in computer technology. Xerox PARC is almost legendary because they assembled many of the great minds in computer systems and their associated technologies,[1] who produced such state-

---

[1] Robert X. Cringely, *Accidental Empires* (Addison Wesley, 1992).

of-the art results as:

1.  Computer architectures
2.  Input devices (such as the "mouse")
3.  The networking of computers
4.  Computer languages (e.g., JaM)
5.  Laser printers

Xerox could have moved into any one or several of these technologies—ahead of their competitors. Instead, they shifted into mostly unrelated fields (e.g., real estate investments), where they lost lots of money. Another tragic example of this kind of mindset is IBM, a longtime American success story. As they transitioned from typewriters into computers where they established a dominant position, they recognized the necessity of software (such as operating systems for their computers), and spent lots of R&D money on developing it. Their fault was in significantly underestimating software's value as a business line. The "vacuum" thus created left an open field for Microsoft to step into, even as the two companies worked together on bringing the IBM PC into the marketplace.

In general, most large successful companies make serious investments in R&D, *and* pay attention to how the results can be put into their day-to-day operations. Actively look for R&D dividends. Listen—and listen hard—to the results and related recommendations. Ignoring R&D findings means a big waste of money and a fast slippery slide into failure for you and your company.

# ADD MORE NEW-START INITIATIVES
# EVERY YEAR—THE MORE THE MERRIER

New initiatives create more excitement, but is there a point where new areas of focus may be counterproductive? They're in the plan, but are they going to be effectively considered in the real world?

We are talking here about strategies, rather than tactics. There may be several shifts in tactics during any particular year. Strategies are meant to be more stable and gradual in their execution, so you can test whether they are actually working as you go along. Many people get caught between the need to make more progress, more quickly, and the need to be patient and watch for results.

A particular adventure in my life relates directly to this matter of strategic initiatives. During the 1980s I became president of a subsidiary of a high-tech company. The subsidiary's revenues were about $80 million, and I was quite anxious to set the new strategic course of the enterprise.[1] During several meetings with my vice presidents, we defined thirty strategic initiatives for the company. Working with a smaller group, we pared down the number of initiatives to fifteen. On my own, I dropped two of

[1] H. Eisner, *Managing Complex Systems–Thinking Outside the Box* (John Wiley, 2005), p. 86.

these, winding up with a total of thirteen new initiatives. I went back to my VPs, and asked for more written detail about how we planned to implement this set of thirteen, which they all provided within a few days. I was then ready to unveil this wonderful plan to my boss, an executive in the parent company.

He studied it for no more than five minutes, and then responded: "I like the write-ups, and their format, but there are clearly too many of them." I asked him to explain. He answered, "For this size company, there is no way you and your people can take on this many new initiatives. You just don't have the resources to get there from here. And I think a better plan is to focus on a fewer number of them, but make sure that you can actually make some significant progress on each one of them."

"I can see your logic," I answered, "but how did you get there so fast?"

His answer was, "Thirty-five years of experience."

Yes, experience goes a long way toward providing answers to this type of question. The size of an enterprise has a lot to do with how many new challenges can be undertaken in a given period of time. Too many of them will just simply not work. There will not be enough success to give everyone a sense of really moving forward. The net result is likely to be frustration rather than progress. That's not what you are looking for.

Be careful not to agree to impossible goals and plans, lest you set the stage for failure rather than success.

# Never Invest in Your "Cash Cows"—You Can Keep Milking Them Forever

A "cash cow" is a line of business that delivers excellent revenues and profits, year after year, and helps to support other, less stable, lines of business. There's an old joke about this cow whose milk supply seemed to dry up. The owner had the cow looked at by several veterinarians, to no avail. Finally, in desperation, he brought a psychiatrist into the fray. The "shrink" spent a couple of private hours with the cow, and finally emerged with a full pail of milk. The owner was ecstatic, but also flabbergasted. "How did you do that?" asked the owner. The shrink replied, "You've been pulling on your cow's teats for years now. Have you ever stopped, for even one moment, to tell her that you loved her?"

Cash cows are wonderful, but they need:
1. Solid maintenance
2. Excellent operators
3. Continuous improvement
4. A certain amount of TLC (see cow story above)
5. Modest investments (e.g., keep feeding the cow)

The folks in charge of the cash cows keep the cash coming in which provides cash to keep building the business. In a very real sense, these folks can keep a cash cow healthy as long as they take care of it—in business that means maintaining the product's quality and upgrading it to meet market conditions.

Cash cow product managers who are doing a very good job want to be well compensated for doing so. They also want the "psychic" income of being recognized, in concrete ways, for their critical importance to the company. They want management to acknowledge that their jobs are not so easy, and that they are dealing properly with certain potential problems. Otherwise—no more happy cash cow tenders.

But let's be realistic. Nothing lasts forever, even cash cows. Many managers do not really appreciate this, and therefore do not actively prolong the life of their cash cows. This can be a very large mistake.

Some years ago, when I was part of the executive team in a systems company, we were reviewing the bid plan on a contract for which we were the incumbent. That contract was one of our cash cows, and we thought we had it made. We had put one of our best and most serious VPs in charge of the contract and the proposal for a renewal. We were all convinced we would win the contract, including the VP in charge of the bid.

Looking back, it is easy to see we were overconfident and did not adequately probe into certain risks. As it turned out, we lost the re-compete. We were "blind-sided" by a very low-cost bid and a few really good new ideas from one of our competitors. We never seriously examined the possibility that our cash cow could die. It was a painful lesson that we all learned. Cash cows are not immortal. It's like the age-old adage: Some aspects of business are not really appreciated until they are gone. Every now and then it's important to stop and consider how to invest in a product or service to keep the milk flowing. Without that investment, the cash cow might die, and send the rest of the company into a tailspin. Before it's too late, how healthy is your best product?

# No One Inside Your Organization Knows as Much as Those Outside It

One of my old bosses, the CEO of the company, believed this adage, and my colleagues and I found it a constant source of aggravation. Any time we lost a contract bid to a competitor, my boss would say something like, "I wish we had their VP in our company, and knew what he seems to know." Yet he gave few kudos to our people when we won a tough competition. Maybe he thought our wins were accidents. This attitude had some real effects on staff morale—all of them negative.

So we had a lot of "outside heroes," according to my boss. We seemed to have approximately zero "inside heroes." This, of course, made no sense when it came time for annual reviews of salaries and bonuses. "How can I be getting a bonus when not once this whole year did I do something special?" Often it was my job to explain this apparent contradiction. If your executives are "tilted" to outside experts versus insiders, as night follows day, you will find that your best people are resentful. They won't simmer forever, but move on to other, more hospitable, enterprises. The true attitudes of your executives "seep" through and the bad ones can poison the well.

In academic environments this kind of "inside-outside" favoritism is particularly dangerous. Usually, a college dean operates through the chairpersons of the various departments to get things done, and has her own office staff and set of administrators to help her. When and if the dean depends primarily on the advice of her staff people—rather than consulting the department chairs—serious problems can arise. First, the "line" department chairs begin to feel they've lost their power and prestige to a set of office workers and administrators. This they will not accept and will fight back fiercely by:

1. Arguing constantly against what the dean wants done and challenging its validity
2. Refusing to discuss the dean's ideas and initiatives with the faculty at large
3. Thwarting the dean's agenda by not acting on it.

This scenario is a killer and will soon lead to a dysfunctional school. The dean will fight back, possibly not realizing that it was she who basically caused the problem. Managing professors requires excellent management skills that academics often do not possess. Many do not understand that the department chairpersons and the professors are the "heart and soul" of the enterprise. If they are alienated, failure is just around the corner. And just about guaranteed.

# ALWAYS SET DIFFICULT "STRETCH" GOALS AND BLAME YOUR PEOPLE WHEN THEY AREN'T MET

"Stretch" goals are an acknowledged part of business, but the question is: How far is the stretch? A stretch that is too far leaves people with no real hope of achieving it, and will lead to "why even try" behavior. A stretch that is reasonable, on the other hand, will be accepted as a challenge worth pursuing—as long as the rewards are perceived to be commensurate with the effort. A good boss (and company) knows exactly how far to try to stretch, leading to highly motivated people and a high likelihood of achieving the stated goals.

We all know that positive rewards motivate folks to try to achieve better results. Threats of unreasonable punishment do not. Putting your people "on the rack" when they fail to meet a stretch goal is not a good idea. It is more likely to lead to protests, with an end game of: "My resignation letter is on your desk."

Of course, we also realize that stretch goals to one person may not be stretches to someone else. When Ross Perot worked for IBM, for instance, he met his goals for the year by the end of January. He tried to negotiate a set of adjusted rewards for the year, but was turned down. Without the prospect of improving his rewards for yet even better performance for the rest of the year, he quit and soon thereafter started his own company, EDS. After selling that enterprise to General Motors for a bundle, he was in a position to do just about anything he wanted, even run for the President of the United States! This Perot story is a different twist on the matter of stretch goals and relates to the possibility that for some folks, it's not really a stretch. They often become presidents of companies. For mere mortals, on the other hand, it is quite unpleasant to miss such goals and then experience the "rack."

To put some numbers on it, let us assume that the likelihood (probability) of making your goals for each year is about 80 percent. In this case, the approximate likelihood that you will *fail to make your goals for at least one* of the next three years is less than 50 percent. As you progress up the corporate ladder, failure to meet goals is less tolerated, especially when your colleagues make theirs, year after year. The "system" tends to be tilted toward success.

So we might summarize by saying that stretch goals can be OK if:

1.  You keep away from draconian consequences
2.  They push underachievers, especially if the whole company is underachieving
3.  Achievers are rewarded generously if the goals are met.

But stretch goals can cause big problems if highly punitive. Just keep in mind that an over-stretch can easily lead to breakage.

# Conduct Only "Virtual" Meetings— All Face-to-Face Meetings Are Too Expensive and Inefficient

It is certainly true that modern technology has replaced the need for some face-to-face meetings. E-mail, voice mail, telephone conversations, telephone conferencing and video teleconferencing (VTC) have become highly efficient communications media and should be used as much as possible, where appropriate. But face-to-face meetings are still important—both internally with co-workers and externally with clients, suppliers, and others.

Harold Geneen, one of America's best managers, set a new high standard for building a strong competitive company. He was a staunch advocate of direct face-to-face meetings, and credited, in his own words, "numerous and frequent" meetings for his success in building ITT from a $766M enterprise to a $16.7B company, over a period of some eighteen years.[1] Indeed, he increased ITT's earnings for fifty-eight consecutive quarters, or fourteen and a half years. To Geneen, face-to-face meetings were a major ingredient in achieving the successes that he and his executives were able to achieve. Even when he expanded the business overseas, he insisted on personal meetings with

---

[1] H. Geneen, with A. Moscow, *Managing* (Avon Books, 1984).

his European directors, watching "the look on a man's face, his tone of voice, (and) his body language" to influence his decisions.

Face-to-face meetings, of course, allow you to "read" how people look, feel, and think. This extends beyond the people in the company to both customers and suppliers. If you are going to extend delivery dates and/or credit to a supplier, you want to trust the person you are dealing with. Face-to-face interactions help you to build trust, or the opposite. If you make a handshake deal with a customer, you want to believe that this person will follow through on the handshake.

Finally, today's world is one in which there is a lot of active and purposeful team building, much of which can be achieved at roundtable meetings. We have learned how to use technology to support such meetings, but they can't replace personal contact. They can only facilitate it.

The costs may be relatively high to get all the key players at a roundtable meeting, but try to envision boards of director meetings by video teleconferencing. Just not good enough. Let's make sure to keep the human element in our enterprises. In many ways, that's what it's all about.

# DON'T BOTHER TO CONGRATULATE YOUR KEY PLAYERS FOR A JOB WELL DONE—SENIOR MANAGERS DON'T NEED COMPLIMENTS

If you accept this statement, you are making a judgment about the *needs* of your employees—especially your key people, many of whom are your senior folks. As mature people who have had numerous work experiences and responsibilities, it's easy to believe that they don't really need an "attaboy" every now and then. Could this be true, or is it violating some deep feeling that you have about the nature of people?

When talking about needs, let's take look at a seminal piece of work called "Maslow's Hierarchy of Needs (HoN)," developed by psychologist Abraham Maslow in his 1943 paper, *A Theory of Human Motivation.* Maslow posited that people's needs fit into the following hierarchy:

1. Physiological
2. Safety
3. Social
4. Esteem
5. Self-actualization

According to this theory, as our needs are satisfied at a lower level on this "ladder, we move up to a higher rung.

For example, social needs become more dominant only when basic safety and physiological needs have been met. In the same way, if social and esteem needs are largely satisfied, a person tends to seek self-actualization.

If we accept Maslow's framework, which is widely cited, we would conclude that most of our employees are in one or the other of the top three needs (i.e., social, esteem, self-actualization). Social needs have to do with positive interactions and affiliations.

Further, this is a necessary "stepping stone" to move on to the esteem and self-actualization needs. Complimenting your key people for a job well done will help them reach the top three levels, in varying degrees, depending upon their current needs. In other words, making an esteemed employee feel good might be helpful, and certainly cannot hurt (assuming it is given sincerely). The point is that all of us have needs, and helping employees satisfy their needs in the workplace is not something that should be capriciously withheld—especially if it is relatively easy to offer.

Just because people are senior, or especially gifted in their work, does not mean that they have automatically checked their psychological needs at the door. And it is a mistake to assume that this is the case. If you are still doubtful, try running a few experiments. Make sure to give several "pats on the back" to those who have done particularly fine work. You may also add the ingredient of public awards for a job well done. Take a good look at the faces of the people receiving these awards. They will, inevitably, be sporting a broad smile. Intrinsic motivation is a wonderful thing. Adding extrinsic motivation makes it even better, no matter who you are. Feelings and thoughts that say, "You are appreciated" can do wonders. Just about everyone wants to feel appreciated.

# GIVE YOUR PEOPLE UNREASONABLE DEADLINES TO PUSH THEIR PRODUCTIVITY

The syndrome of the unreasonable schedule, also called the "Land of the Off-the-wall Deadline (LOD)," can take hold when the perpetrator has one or more of the following mindsets:

1. Pushing hard on schedules leads to a highly disciplined organization where people understand the critical necessity of meeting those deadlines, and get used to it.

2. Meeting very stringent schedules gives those who achieve them a strong sense of accomplishment and well-being.

3. When large numbers of people in your company complete taxing schedules on time, you achieve higher productivity levels, i.e., more is accomplished within a given time period.

4. As a consequence of (3) above, you will tend to beat your competition a larger percentage of the time.

Although there may well be an element of truth in all of the above, this overall practice can also lead to lots of anger, burnout, and high rates of turnover. People tend to accept difficult schedules when and if they see a clear need for doing so. A good example is when a customer requires early delivery for a particular piece of work. Without a clear need, people will not generally accept a steady diet of long hours. For families especially, when Mommy or Daddy is working all the time, life is hard and stressful. What does the family have to do with running an effective and efficient business? Answer: Plenty.

Another approach to scheduling has to do with the notion of "reserves." For many projects that are considered "high risk," each layer of management feels compelled to establish a "reserve." If three layers of management each keep a 10 percent reserve in schedule, then the project leader is "forced" to try to complete the project in about 73 percent of the original timeline. Question: Is that reasonable? Answer: Sometimes, but not often.

Would a different approach make more sense? The answer is "yes" and it involves having each employee define when he or she is able to complete a given assignment. After the boss reviews all of these inputs, the estimates are accepted or adjusted, based upon several factors, such as:

▶ Overall true needs of the aggregate set of tasks
▶ History of each employee, especially with respect to meeting schedules
▶ A discussion between boss and employee as to the nature of each assignment
▶ The extent to which timelines might be decreased, or met, through the addition of more people, working together.

This "participative" approach to setting schedules is a step in the direction of true problem solving, and likely to lead to better reactions and results.

# Give Generous Bonuses to Your Executives—Whether They Meet Company and Personal Goals … or Not

We seem to have entered a period when business executives expect outrageous salaries, bonuses, and stock options. You hear talk about gigantic remuneration "packages" that include all medical services, automobiles, club memberships, and more. It's almost as if there were no reason for an executive to ever pay for anything out of his or her own pocket.

In 1987, a movie by the name of *Wall Street* predicted all too well where we, as a nation, were headed. At an important and well-attended meeting, Michael Douglas's character, Gordon Gekko, tells us what it's all about. The word is "greed," and he declares greed to be an exceedingly good thing. This perspective, unfortunately, seems to have been adopted by too many of our business folk.

In 2006, CEOs were making 431 times more than the average line worker in a company—compared with a "multiplier" of 142 in 1994.[1] Looking at some numbers—in 1994 an average worker made $40,000 per year while the CEO

[1] Rana Foroohar, "Are They Worthy?" *Newsweek Magazine*, September 2006.

made $5.7 million. Today the CEO makes around $17.2 million per year, about a three-fold increase. Does that seem fair and equitable to you? So the question becomes, if you're in a position to make these types of decisions, what would you try to do?

If your answer is to give outrageous "packages," you are also supporting unbridled greed in the organization. Before long, it's all about money, and not about what the company does, or what it makes, or how it maintains quality, or what it stands for. When it's only about money, any organization will start down that slippery slope toward failure.

To make the current situation even more obscene, total remuneration is often not keyed, in ways that can be measured, to the performance of the company. Revenues and profits drop, and guess what— the executives enter the next year with even greater "packages." After all, "contracts" call for ever-increasing remuneration, except when the executive can be fired "for cause." You know what a person has to do to be fired for cause? Yes, you do, so I don't have to repeat it here.

Superior performance on the job is what it's all about. Please keep that in mind when it comes time each year to award bonuses and stock options. Let's try to make it real so that employees agree that management has it right. Let's not struggle in December to articulate management by objective goals, then throw it all away at the end of the year when performance is poor, and the rationale is "but if we do that, so-and-so will be unhappy." How about making the shareholders and ordinary employees happy?

# 21

# Take On a Difficult New Project and Hire the Ten Smartest People in the Country to Lead It

As with most of the other "imperatives" cited in this book, on first reading it makes a lot of sense. Further, there is at least one success story that can be cited for which this approach was taken. And, with some deeper thought, it is likely that a few others may be recalled (e.g., from the field of cryptology and code-breaking).

The clear success story is the Manhattan Project, established in the 1940s to produce the first atom bomb for the United States. The civilian head of this project was Robert Oppenheimer, well respected as both a scientist and an administrator. Choosing a leader of lesser qualifications would likely have led to major problems. On the military side, the leader was General Leslie R. Groves. He was by no means the "smartest," but he understood his role as a facilitator and remover of barriers. And he executed that role very well. He did not try to second-guess the special and elite project team. Rather, he respected them and tried to help them.

Beyond Oppenheimer, the technical depth of the team was perhaps the strongest ever assembled. The theory of building such a bomb was well understood. But many obstacles lay ahead, and many real-world practical problems had to be solved. The team was up to this

challenge, and the overall project was clearly an outstanding success.

So what's the problem with trying to do a very difficult job by hiring the smartest people in the world? Try
these:

1.  The people have not worked together before, and
    therefore will not operate as a true team.
2.  The new hires may well challenge each other in-
    definitely for intellectual supremacy.
3.  They may also challenge the decisions made by
    whoever is put in charge.
4.  They will not easily accept one person as the
    "boss."
5.  Since their market attractiveness is high, they
    will always be prepared to "walk" if they don't
    like what's going on.
6.  They may lose interest in the problem they were
    brought in to solve, and start off in a different
    direction, and
7.  A few other negatives that go along with trying
    to "manage" exceptionally smart folks.

# If You're in Hardware, Don't Venture into Software

You've been making money in a hardware-oriented business (like planes, trains, and automobiles) for lots of years without worrying about software. Why start worrying about it now?

Some business folks have argued that there are enough problems to go around just dealing with hardware. It's been the distinguishing feature for decades. Customers buy automobiles, and appliances, and houses on the basis of how they look, and how well they work. Iacocca proved it with the Mustang, Maytag proved it with their washers and dryers, and Levitt proved it in housing. I'm in a similar business, and I don't need much software. So here again, why start worrying about it now?

If you're not in the business of software, the whole topic seems elusive. After all, it has no physical substance, and you can't weigh it, smell it, or touch it. My engineering background tells me then that it may not really exist.

And the answer is: Wake up to the new reality. It does exist, and may be the pivotal factor in the success or failure of your hardware-oriented business—right now, and into the future. It will affect you until the day of your retirement, and beyond that.

So let's take a very brief look at areas in which software is seriously affecting hardware and other business areas:

- ► Automobiles have more and more controlling software,
- ► Telephone systems rely on software for tracking calls all over the world,
- ► Computer software controls many types of manufacturing processes,
- ► The Internet is driven by software,
- ► Small businesses of all varieties do inventory control with software systems,
- ► Human resources departments keep track of people using software,
- ► Hospitals and healthcare providers create and convey information using software, and
- ► How many more can you add to this list, including your own business?

Yes, the world of software is here to stay, even if you produce only nuts and bolts.

In May 2004, the Second National Software Security Summit addressed the "software issue"[1] in its many dimensions, and released its summit report the next April. Their articulated National Software Strategy pointed to four main areas for deeper consideration and solution:

1. Improving software trustworthiness
2. Educating and fielding the software workforce
3. Re-energizing software research and development
4. Encouraging innovation within the US software industry.

So what can you do, as a small or large business, in hardware or otherwise, to have software help you rather than adopt a policy of benign neglect? Hire your first CSO (Corporate Software Officer) and give him or her some resources as well as your ear.

---

[1] Center for National Software Studies, "Software 2015," April 29, 2005.

# MAKE SURE YOUR DIRECT REPORTS DON'T LEAVE WORK BEFORE YOU DO

There are a few enterprises (maybe more than a few) where hours worked are almost as important as what is produced —a prime example being businesses where employees generate "billable hours." And, perhaps, you think billable hours are best developed in the office, rather than at home or conferencing in the local bowling alley with a customer. Statistics are hard to come by in this area.

When I was part of the professional services industry, it was well known that companies X, Y, and Z operated this way. It was a seriously bad idea to leave the office before your boss, many of whom brought in a sandwich for dinner and didn't go home before eight or nine p.m. Of course, many didn't have anyone to go home to.

The stakes were clear. If you put in the hours, you had a shot at VP or partner. If you didn't, your chances were miniscule. And after you were properly rewarded, some years later, you were not inclined to change the rules for others. You'd jumped all the hurdles, so why argue with success?

There are many companies that think differently. For them, it's about trust and getting the right results— not just about putting in the hours. And if, in a particular case, hours are critical to getting the job done, then employees are trusted to get it done well by managing their own hours. Many trusted employees do lots of work at home, after dinner, and after spending some time with the family. Just because you can't see your employee at 8:30 p.m. in the office, doesn't mean there's no work being done at home.

David Packard, co-founder of computer giant Hewlett-Packard (HP), made sure the "HP Way" was flat-out trust in their employees. In his 1995 book with that title,[1] he devotes a full chapter to how he and his co-founder, Bill Hewlett, went about developing this high level of trust between employees and management. It is refreshing to see how a company can maintain a trusting attitude over a period of many, many decades—despite recent unfortunate missteps by a few HP executives.

Often it comes down to trust, coupled with demonstrable results. Professionals should be treated in a professional manner. At the same time, professionals must understand how to "fit in" with the established culture. And cultures that engender lack of trust need to be examined in the light of current best practices. Best practices can be very flexible as well as built on trust. People will respond to and rally around corporate cultures that stand for respect for each individual. And they will come out on the negative side when the boss expects you to put in every minute of overtime hours in order to be successful.

Want a good set of principles and answers? Try the "HP Way."

[1] David Packard, *The HP Way* (Harper Business, 1995).

24

# ALWAYS TRUST YOUR STAFF PEOPLE MORE THAN YOUR LINE ORGANIZATION

As suggested in chapter 15, when you only listen to what your staff tells you and ignore those "on the line," your organization can soon become dysfunctional. Of course, you, like many managers in similar circumstances, may not realize that it's your fault this organizational unraveling started in the first place.

A simple example: the Secretary of Defense (SECDEF) is a line position with thousands of people (not to mention equipment) under his command. On the other hand, the National Security Advisor (NSA) is a very high-level staff position. Typically, the President will ask for the advice of both persons. If the advice on a given issue is the same, then there is no problem. However, if the advice is often different, *and* the President almost always agrees with the NSA, then big problems are right around the corner. The SECDEF will be very aware that the President is not listening to him, and a blow-up of some kind is more-or-less inevitable. In this case, the staff advisor is most likely to be at risk. Such is life, and this problem is not a neat or simple one.

So, you've got to recognize that your line organization is the "backbone" of your enterprise. They've got the resources (e.g., people, etc.) to mobilize to get things done.

These resources, depending upon the size of the overall organization, can easily number hundreds (or thousands) of people with a wide variety of backgrounds and skills. They've also been given the responsibility, authority, and power to carry out projects in their area. Presumably, you meant it to be that way when you hired them and established the organization's structure.

In contrast, the staff person reporting to you may have a secretary (and possibly no one else) reporting to him or her. Other resources may have to be borrowed, from time to time. These staff folks operate largely as advisors to you, on issues that you select.

Having a good solid group of staff people reporting to you is a distinct asset. But if you are giving more weight to their inputs and advice than to your line people, you are creating a serious problem, and you're part of the problem.

Avoid playing the "blame game." Figure out what to do, and do it. But do not undermine the authority of your line organization. Get a different line manager, if necessary, but be clear about how you contributed to the difficulty. And, when in doubt, remember the old cliché that often works: Re-organize, one more time.

Select your staff advisors with great care since they must understand how vulnerable their position might be. They need to keep a low profile and be extremely circumspect in how they give their advice. They also need to be strong team players who can keep their egos under wraps and not worry about who gets the credit. People like this are not so easy to find.

# 25
# Don't Buy into Continuous Improvement Since Best Is Often the Enemy of Good Enough

Some people are adamant that "if it ain't broke, don't fix it." If it ain't broke usually means "it's working and we're making money doing it that way."

Of course, that may be true, but working okay now does not necessarily mean it will be working okay tomorrow. Consider the example of Wang Laboratories, a multibillion-dollar company that was doing extremely well in 1988, but by 1993 had filed for bankruptcy because they hadn't seen the changes coming in word processing hardware and software.

There are many other examples of companies that didn't see it coming. How about Apollo, DEC, and SDS in the computer field? Even IBM had a significant blind spot when they underestimated the importance of software, and conceded part of that world to Microsoft. And how about Xerox when they more-or-less completely disregarded the wonderful results that were coming from their Palo Alto Research Center?

Continuous improvement (CI) suggests a longterm view with a strategy of steady improvement of products and processes. "Product" improvement often focuses on quality, as advocated by all Total Quality Management (TQM) initiatives. "Process" improvement was the emphasis

49

of the Business Process Reengineering (BPR) theory that burst into corporate consciousness via the blockbuster book by Hammer and Champy [1] [1]Note the word "process" in the center of that triad.

Continuous improvement is a more-or-less surefire way to move from average to good, from good to better, and from better to best. Each step usually results in improved revenues and profits.

It also produces a mindset that says: "We always care about doing better." Not to care about getting better is often the first step toward a downward trajectory in the marketplaces. The best business leaders agree that we must always be moving forward (like sharks). As pitcher Satchel Paige once said about his beloved game of baseball, "Don't look back, they may be gaining on you."

At the same time, we must acknowledge that, from time to time, we are truly re-arranging the deck chairs on the Titanic. We are "fine-tuning," leading to diminishing returns and a misplaced sense of priorities. We are working on the unimportant problems, and missing the big picture problems that could make the difference between success and failure. All of that can and does happen, and is clearly to be avoided. But a good company can manage to do both—make tactical continuous improvements and keep a few folks looking out for icebergs. The trick then becomes being seriously able to listen to both, when the alarm bell sounds from several directions.

A CEO friend clearly defined this ability: "That's why we have two ears," he exclaimed. "So we can hear both alarms, each with the proper sense of urgency."

[1] M. Hammer & J. Champy, *Reengineering the Corporation* (Harper Business, 1993).

# Always Do What Your Customer Wants You To Do

I remember clearly, though it was many years ago, the cover of *Business Week* that featured a customer with a crown on his head. The message was—finally, in business, we have realized that the "customer is king." Now all enterprises bow to their customer.

But wait just a minute. Customers are indeed very important. Some like to create the impression that they can walk on water. Some may even walk around with crowns on their heads. However, even kings can be wrong. Even kings have been deposed. Even kings do not qualify as god-like (though some may believe and behave otherwise).

In today's highly diversified world, there are many kinds of customers. Some are excellent, some are terrible, and many are in between. They are likely to form the usual bell-shaped curve with: 2.5 percent are excellent customers at the top, and 2.5 percent are absolutely terrible customers at the bottom. If you listen only to what this demanding 2.5 percent want, your organization could get into serious trouble.

Here are some of the ways that your customer might lead you astray:

1. Request that you back off from your usual product quality
2. Request that you "doctor" your invoices in unacceptable ways
3. Demand that you provide some kind of "kickback"
4. Lead you to make a bad business decisions under some type of "threat"
5. Treat you with anything less than respect
6. Do something that violates your commitment to a solid and positive set of ethical principles.

And lots of others can be added to this list.

Recognize, also, that you are seeking a strictly business relationship with all your customers—good and bad. Be dependent upon each other for business, but in healthy ways. Be aware of boundaries that need to be kept, and not crossed.

So it's true that customers are very important, but they also come and go. If and when they cross the line, and ask for something in the list above, it's time for them to go. This might create a hardship for you; but if you have a solid company, you will likely survive a short-term loss. Tying your fortune to a "terrible" customer can ruin your reputation as well as your company. And don't believe it can't happen to you. Many folks now behind bars thought their customer was right, no matter what.

# MIDWORD

We've now reached the midway point in our exploration of wrong ways to do things in your company. I'm sure you haven't agreed with all my failure points so far; but for me, that's a good sign. It shows me that I have uncovered some very real pitfalls in any business. Now I want you to be thinking, as you read, "Wait a minute. Let me chew on that for a while longer." The extra thinking will get you where you want to go—especially as the world around us keeps changing. After all, what was wisdom thirty years ago, might not make much sense today.

There are 26 suggestions for helping to sink your enterprise up to this point. Another 26 will follow. At this midpoint I would like to list my "top ten" from the first list of 26. Compare mine with your "top ten:"

1. After laboring over your strategic plan, ignore it for a year.
2. Hire smart folks, then don't listen to them.
5. Shift exclusively to growth by acquisition when your organic growth bogs down.
6. Meetings take key managers away from their real work.
10. If the process is right, the resulting product will be right.
14. Never invest in your "cash cows"—you can keep milking them forever.

15.  No one inside your organization knows as much as those outside it.
16.  Always set difficult "stretch" goals and blame your people when they aren't met.
20.  Give generous bonuses to your executives— whether they meet company and personal goals … or not
26.  Always do what your customer wants you to do.

In scanning this list, I find no particular pattern. I've considered whether I ought to re-order all 52 of the suggestions so that a pattern emerges from the first 26. Upon further reflection, I've held my ground. Maybe a certain amount of randomness is a good thing. Ultimately, each suggestion stands on its own, or fails to do so. And the consequences are what they are.

Before we continue with suggestions 27 through 52, let me say one more thing. Just about every time I have the good fortune to read the words of our most outstanding managers, I find that they say, in one way or another: "I've learned more from my mistakes than I have from my best decisions." Given my roughly twenty years as a manager in industry, I would have to echo that conclusion. If you are paying attention, and are truly honest as well, it's the mistakes you remember, as well as the consequences of those mistakes. For many, really nasty consequences are just about impossible to forget. Hopefully, they cut down on the future error rate. And they also keep us learning and adjusting. Let's not make that mistake again!

# LOWER PRICE IS ALWAYS THE WINNING STRATEGY

It is certainly true that many enterprises have done well following this strategy. One, of course, has been Wal-Mart, although many have criticized their low-price approach for driving smaller enterprises out of business—a very negative consequence. Michael Dell of Dell Computer, on the other hand, has built a very successful company with a strategy that combines low price with low overhead costs. It remains to be seen whether or not this strategy will continue to be successful.

The large automakers seem to have reserved a spot for a low price strategy with their subcompacts, built in response to higher gasoline prices and demand for fuel efficiency. When fuel costs are high, many people simply can't afford higher automobile prices.

There are, indeed, many other examples of a low price approach to the market, such as COSTCO, Sam's Club, and the Burlington Coat Factory. But, at the same time, examples of the opposite approach are plentiful. One domain in which one sees high prices valued is in designer clothing and accessories. Nordstrom's was successful with this strategy even while entering an overcrowded market. Peters and Waterman could not stop raving about this firm in their classic book, *In Search of Excellence*.[1] Higher prices can be seen at Saks Fifth Avenue, Gucci's, and even Bloomingdale's, all of which appear to be doing well in this market. This is true even though they have to contend with firms such Filene's Basement that is able to focus on the "lower end," as is Target.

So—what is one to make of all this? Is lower price always a winning strategy? The answer is clearly "no" as we see living, breathing examples of both high price and low price approaches working in their own markets. And what is it that allows the high prices to be acceptable to so many consumers? The answer, mainly, lies in two words: service and quality. If we add "style," for lots of clothing and automobiles, we have covered most of the waterfront. Just keep in mind that setting up a BMW or Bentley dealership in a poor neighborhood is not likely to lead to great success.

So let's summarize by highlighting three words: service, quality, and style. If you can offer all three, you are likely to be able to sell at higher prices and still appeal to many consumers. It can take a delicate touch to find the right offerings at prices that make a profitable enterprise. Target's strategy is to combine style with lower prices, and it seems to be working.

Now, one last complication as we examine the real estate industry where three other words rule pricing structure. This factor was alluded to earlier, although somewhat obliquely. Many associate that factor with real estate, but it can also be applied in a broader context. You hear it everywhere expressed in the three words: location, location, location.

---

[1] T. Peters and R. Waterman, *In Search of Excellence* (Harper & Row, 1982).

# PLANS AREN'T OFTEN FOLLOWED, SO IT'S MORE-OR-LESS FUTILE TO PLAN

Many managers feel a certain frustration with plans and planning. They often go through elaborate and time-consuming strategic and tactical planning processes—only to find that when the bell goes off, all plans become obsolete. Some use the acronym "OBE," meaning "overtaken by events." Those events often start as soon as the planning cycle is over and you proceed into implementation. In that phase, the troops do what they did before—even if the plan says we have deliberately changed our direction and our action plan.

Is it true that plans are often not followed? The answer appears to be "yes." However, it is also true that good planning is highly correlated with success. I've heard it said that if you don't know where you're going, any path will get you there (wherever "there" is). That appears also to be true, but is it any way to run a company, or a division within a company?

If you are taking the time and expending the energy to do solid planning, and the plans are not being followed, you have a situation that needs to be addressed. The chain of command has a serious weakness, and that may be you or one of your reports. You need to ask yourself some questions about the aftermath of planning, such as:

1. Do you measure progress against the plan?
2. Do you tend not to measure progress at all?
3. Do you inadvertently show that the plan need not be followed, as long as your people keep you informed?
4. Do you let your direct reports violate the plan, even after you have declared how important the plan is?
5. Are you, in any way, sabotaging your own plan?

Answering these types of questions will help you zero in on why your plans may not be followed.

Conventional project management lore confirms that there are at least three distinct steps that need to be taken after the planning work has been done. These steps are the following:[1]

1. Organizing
2. Directing, and
3. Monitoring

If there are weak spots in any of the above post-planning activities, your plan may represent paper only, with little or no execution. That's a problem that needs fixing. And it's you that needs to take the lead in doing so. If you fail to do so, you're likely taking another step *down* the ladder of success.

[1] H. Eisner, *Essentials of Project and Systems Engineering Management*, 2nd ed. (John Wiley, 2002).

# MICROMANAGE AVERAGE OR LESS-THAN-AVERAGE PERFORMERS TO GET THEM TO PRODUCE

This premise appears quite plausible. As you deal with employees who are less and less competent, it is necessary to resort to more and more micromanagement, a much maligned practice. Yes, it is plausible, but is it really true? By behaving as if it were true, are we helping or hurting the people and the organization?

I contend that the premise is largely incorrect, based upon my own life experiences and readings. How can this be the case? Well, it turns out that people like to be challenged by their work, at whatever their level of performance and competence. Challenging assignments and micromanagement generally do not fit well together. Responding to a challenge is a long way from having your hand held every step of the way. So, with some minor exceptions, we have to put micromanagement back where it belongs—mostly on the junk heap of yesterday's as well as today's management practices.

Micromanagement is not only a less-than-wonderful imposition on the worker, it is also a burden for the manager. By spending lots of extra time with the less-than-average performer, how can managers get their own jobs done? They probably cannot do so, meaning that the micromanager is doing some damage to the manager as well as the managed. Not really a good thing.

Instead of micromanaging, is there a better approach? The answer is distinctly "yes." It lies in such words and actions as guidance, facilitation, training (i.e., formal and OJT), as well as education (i.e., college courses). This approach gives people a chance to obtain help at whatever their level, and within well-recognized and accepted venues and contexts. For example, getting a BS in engineering will prepare people for solving lots of engineering-type problems. Moving on from there, an MBA may well convert a below-average performer into an above-average one. Specialized training for groups of people inside a company will almost always lift the performance of everyone in the group. And learning side-by-side with peers removes many negatives that are otherwise present in the micromanagement scenario.

In any organization, there are people who will perform in ways that are considered average and below average, as compared with other people in that organization. Generally, these folks are not in need of micromanagement. They are in need of professional help that will give them the skills and motivation to raise their levels of performance. They are in need of an organized approach to helping them do better, from people who are trained to help in this type of situation.

Perhaps an old and well-known idea is appropriate in this connection. Curiously, it has to do with fishing. The saying behind the idea is: "Give a man a fish, and he has a meal for today. Teach a man how to fish and he has a meal for every day."

Many problems are solved or mitigated through well-conceived education and training.

# You Don't Need SWOT Analysis (Strengths-Weaknesses-Opportunities-Threats)—It Just Slows Down Your Strategic Planning

Maybe you think SWOT analysis, originally proposed by George Steiner,[1] slows down your strategic planning process. And you are right, in a way, because eliminating this analysis of company strengths, weaknesses, opportunities, and threats, will certainly shorten and simplify your planning process. It will also place the planner in considerable peril and can lead to a plan whose essential strategy might well be 180 degrees from where it needs to be. A strategic plan that is done honestly seeks to find the right strategic direction, rather than justify a direction already chosen. It's not supposed to be, for example:

- ▶ We've already decided to diversify, or
- ▶ We've already decided to de-centralize, or
- ▶ We've already decided to enter the telecommunications field (pick your poison).

And now we need a strategic plan that justifies these choices, and shows how they're to be executed in the

[1] G. Steiner, *Strategic Planning* (The Free Press, 1979).

best possible way. No, that's not it.

To illustrate, we are going to omit the SWOT analysis and assume we're doing the strategic planning for Wang Laboratories in the late 1980s. Here's what we *failed* to focus on:

▶ **Strengths**
o   **S.1**–We have the lion's share of the word processing (WP) market, both hardware and software.
o   **S.2**–We have the financial strength to assure our WP position, assuming the market maintains its current trends.

▶ **Weaknesses**
o   **W.1**–We are not really prepared for open computer technology.
o   **W.2**–We are not really able to supply superior WP software for open computer systems.

▶ **Opportunities**
o   **O.1**–We have the wherewithal to sustain our market position by investing in open computer systems and their WP software.
o   **O.2**–We can form strategic alliances if there is a shift to open hardware and software.
o   **O.3**–We have the resources to purchase key hardware and software companies in case of a market shift to open systems.

▶ **Threats**
o   **T.1**–Open source hardware and software in WP represents a critical threat.

Lurking in the above hypothetical statements are clues to useful actions that Wang might have taken at that time.

It would have been most interesting to be a fly on the wall as Dr. Wang and his executives made their business and technology decisions in the late 1980s.

So it may be conjectured that an honest and in-depth SWOT analysis might have helped to keep Wang from going into bankruptcy. Other events that could possibly have benefited from a deeper SWOT investigation include: (a) IBM's failure to see software as a critical business area, (b) Xerox's misadventures with their Palo Alto Research Center, and (c) The merger between Time Warner and AOL. Hindsight, as they say, is both wonderful and 20/20.

# Always Give Your Special Job-Well-Done Rewards in Private

Perhaps this is the one of the most accepted positions in industry: Out-of-cycle raises, bonuses, stock awards and options, certificates of accomplishment, unusual perks, and other special rewards should be given to deserving employees in private. This was how we did it at the company I spent most of my time with, and it seemed to be effective. Of course, we also had nothing to compare it to.

Some years later I became associated with a different company. What I discovered was that they had carefully established both "private" and "public" reward events. Some rewards were given in private, but others at formal celebrations, sometimes with food, sometimes with just wine and cheese, varying in length from one to three hours. For a sit-down dinner variety, spouses were also invited. After the dinner, the awards ceremony proceeded.

At these ceremonies, vice presidents and the president made announcements for all to hear:

> And Jenny receives a superior performance certificate and award for the contributions she made to writing a winning proposal to our most important customer. Jenny, please come up to receive your well-deserved award.

Jenny did so, and all could see that the company valued Jenny and what she had done for the company. Jenny's husband was beaming, and he could not have been more pleased and proud. It was a "public" event, and, at that moment, Jenny was the star and everyone knew it. And many must have thought: "Maybe I'll be the one getting a special award at our next quarterly. I really feel I've got a shot at it, if I . . ."

This type of celebration showed me something I'd forgotten. Public recognition really goes a long way toward creating happy, motivated employees. I've been told that many companies (e.g., IBM) had this mode of behavior highly developed and tuned to perfection. But that was hearsay. When I saw Jenny (and the others) get their rewards, along with public recognition, the reality came home to me. This really works!

So for me, the bottom line goes something like this. Make a long list of all the types of rewards that are available in your company. Then, for each one, carefully define whether they should be given in private or public. And within these two, write down the particulars of presentation. You may decide that most of the numbers (how many dollars) will be kept private. But the fact that one person or another is getting a special award is to be announced to as many people as possible. Try to visualize the ecstatic look on Jenny's husband's face when Jenny was recognized in "public" for the good work she'd done. The glow of that special moment lasts a very long time.

# KEEP YOUR BOSS HONEST BY CHALLENGING JUST ABOUT EVERYTHING HE OR SHE SAYS

Some employees, for reasons that are not particularly clear, see it as part of their job to "keep the boss honest." This is not "honest" in the literal sense, of course. It is acting as if he or she is the guardian of truth, as the employee perceives it. So when the boss tries to make a case that is shaky, the employee sees that as an opportunity to make sure there is no sloppy thinking going on. Some folks do this with a sense of glee that might otherwise be expressed as a "gotcha." The more "gotchas," the greater the contribution to the firm's well being.

When the boss is challenged at every turn, however, his reaction is not likely to be favorable (to understate the obvious). From time to time, challenging someone else may be acceptable, perhaps even illuminating. Pointing out that the boss is wrong most of the time, will not be appreciated.

Now we do have to make a distinction between private and public interactions between manager and subordinate. If a challenge is made in private, the boss may be inclined to at least listen. A lot has to do with the specific language used, and all of the verbal and non-verbal messages. A mature boss may see a one-on-one situation as conducive to clearing the air. And lots of reactions are possible, for example:

1. "I find your attacks on me extremely unpleasant."
2. "It's not your job here to challenge me on every matter that comes up."
3. "If you continue with your unfounded and very annoying criticism of me, I will certainly, and perhaps shortly, have you searching for another job."

Reactions to the above may take many forms. Most of them are likely to be unsatisfactory. Your best reaction might be something like:

"I didn't really understand how strongly you feel about my challenges. I'm truly sorry, and I will stop these challenges immediately."

If the challenger tries instead to explain the whys and wherefores of his position, he or she is likely to be out of a job within the month.

However harsh the above reactions appear to be, see what happens when your challenges are made at public meetings or in front of customers. So-called public challenges may lead to exponential reactions and essentially immediate loss of employment.

I was a witness to this type of scenario only once in my thirty years in industry. A vice president was the challenger, and he could not resist finding flaws in the logic and actions of more senior VPs, and even the president. Eventually and predictably, his seniors ganged up on him on this matter and sent him packing.

There are many times, in business, when attitude becomes the over-riding consideration. Just about all bosses value being treated with simple respect. They do not react well to attempts to keep them "honest." Surprised? It's still the human condition that dominates and carries the day.

# ON-THE-JOB TRAINING IS MOST EFFECTIVE, SO DON'T INVEST IN OUTSIDE TRAINING OR EDUCATION

It is true that on-the-job training (OJT) can be more specific and focused since it is usually comes out of the jobs people are already doing for your organization. This type of training can be informal or formal. For the former, the employee is given opportunities to learn new things related directly to his or her current job (usually). For the latter, employees attend briefing sessions or the like that have been designed for the specific job (usually). Some forms of OJT are directed toward the *next* job for an employee, so as to facilitate the movement from the current job to a very specific next job. Without splitting hairs, OJT tends to be "job" focused, and as such can be extremely helpful. The question may then be asked: "Yes, OJT can be excellent, but is it enough?"

It is the general consensus that OJT is just not enough. Employees are looking for education and training support, and companies are indeed providing these types of opportunities. Not to do so is to fail to be competitive, and your prospective new hire will often use this factor to make a job choice. Not to do so is to send a message to all potential employees that the company does not value a more educated and more highly trained staff.

Education and training, in addition to OJT, are indeed provided by most companies. Conventional education tends to support new credentials such as a bachelor's or master's degree. What one learns there is often not specifically job-related, but allows the employee to become more capable and knowledgeable in a broader context. This perspective may make the employee eligible for a future job, and encourages advancement from within.

I was fortunate, during my thirty years in industry, to have received some amount of OJT, as well as support for education and training. The company partly paid for my graduate education which helped me to obtain a doctorate in engineering and applied science. When I was promoted to a manager position, the company sent me out of the building to go through a management training program. There is no doubt in my mind that this formal management training helped me to become a better manager.

A well-known book by Peter Senge[1] talks about the "learning organization." His concept is so strongly endorsed by industry that many enterprises believe they won't survive unless they support education for their employees. Management needs to embrace this notion, *without* reservation, and *with* dollars and time. Talking about the wonderful OJT opportunities available in the company won't do it these days. Investing sometimes huge amounts of money for qualified employees to get a doctorate or an MBA, along with the time to do so, can make the difference in attracting and holding onto these valuable people in a highly competitive market. If your company is not doing it, you may be on the road to extinction.

---

[1] P. Senge, *The Fifth Discipline—The Art and Practice of the Learning Organization* (DoubledayCurrency, 1990)

# Don't Do Any Contingency Planning
# Since Contingencies Rarely Occur

Contingencies may well be few and far between. But you might think differently if we simply said: Have a primary Plan A, and a backup Plan B. In fact, if you simply asked the question, "What's your Plan B?" just about everyone will know what you mean. Of course, Plan B is the contingency plan.

Another way to define and explore contingencies is to start with the question "What if?" This can be: "What if Plan A doesn't work, what do we do then?" So "what ifs" are an integral part of contingency planning.

Managers are taught, very early in their careers, to ask a lot of questions. They are being briefed all the time, by other lower level managers and by project folks. They know, in advance, that it's their job to see both the strengths as well as the weaknesses of each and every briefing. Their questions are designed to see both, but especially to recognize weaknesses that might "sink the ship." Looking for fatal flaws remains the order of the day, every day.

The questions they ask are frequently "what if" queries:

▶ What if your assumptions are wrong?
▶ What if your customer is negative on the idea?
▶ What if Company X refuses to team with us?

▶   What if we simply cannot staff up to the required
    levels?
▶   What if they won't budge on the cited profit on
    our contract?

All of these are "what ifs."
All of them call for Plan B
All of them require one or more contingency plans.

When you look at it this way, contingency plans are a way to do business just about every day.

Harold Geneen[1], known for his intense and frequent meetings, one after another, was a master at asking the right questions and insisting on honest answers. You lost serious points if you did not have a Plan B when he demanded, "What if that course of action fails?" And he might well have gone on to Plans C and D to see how you thought and how deep you were. Vice Presidents, under Geneen at ITT, in order to survive (and prosper) trained themselves for a host of contingency plans. They went out and spread the Gospel according to Geneen.

And Geneen is not the only one who knew how to ask the right "what if?" questions. Take a look also at Welsh, Iacocca, and Augustine. You'll never again get a case of heartburn when you're asked to do contingency planning.

---

[1] H. Geneen, with A. Moscow, *Managing* (Avon Books, 1984).

# Make Managers Out Of Your
# Best Individual Performers

This particular practice sounds logical, but it can lead to at least two potentially serious problems. By "forcing" your best performers into the role of managers, you may be pushing some square pegs into round holes, who are not likely to be or to become good managers. They will probably settle into the confines and safety of their office, and focus in on individual work. The door will be closed to discourage other people from coming in. The secretary will be instructed to make appointments, preferably tomorrow or the next day. Trust me—I've seen it. The new "manager's" attitude is, "Leave me alone for awhile so I can get some work done." The direct reports are saying, "We never get even a couple of moments alone with him (or her)."

And meetings? Few and far between. The new manager breaks out in a rash if the word meeting is even mentioned, much less happening. "We don't need to be wasting our time chewing on non-problems over and over again. Everyone has an assignment, and should be spending a maximum amount of time carrying out that assignment in the best possible way. That's what I do, and that's what you should be doing." When asked about this point, the answer comes back: "I lead by example, not by meaningless 'feel good' meetings."

These types of managers are almost certain to carve out a juicy portion of the work for themselves. If the team consists of ten people and the manager, the latter will reserve at least a tenth of the direct work for personal attention. And that self-assignment will have first priority, whatever the problems being faced by the other team members, and become a serious source of frustration for some of them.

One reason why the excellent individual performer will accept the offer to be a manager is simply that it is usually a route to higher total remuneration. He reasons: "Clearly I can do both, and I will make more money in the bargain." And he's usually correct in that reasoning. But you wind up with a manager who's not really doing the job. Then what?

A solution to this problem is to establish a promotion path in the company on which excellent individual performers can become vice presidents, without also having to be managers. Chief Technical Officer (CTO) is an example of this specialist non-manager kind of pathway. And the overall remuneration is just a little less than the typical "line manager" executive.

A second problem that can come from moving happy specialists into management positions is that by doing so you may prevent another very capable management-oriented person from having the job. With the door perceived as now shut, he or she may seek employment elsewhere. Thus we have one "solution" leading to two new problems. Not the best way to go.

# IGNORE PERSONNEL PROBLEMS

This is truly a difficult area since you can't always tell how close a personnel problem is to explosion. But like certain aspects of international diplomacy, an explosion is to be avoided, most of the time.

If you wait for the explosion to occur, like Humpty Dumpty, putting the pieces back together again is highly problematic. Too many pieces may be broken and irretrievable.

So one question is: As a manager, how do you know when and how to intercede? The answer depends upon the nature of the personnel problem. Let's take a look at a few possible cases.

**1. Two of your employees are clearly not getting along with each other**. They snipe at and insult one another at every opportunity, including open meetings.

This type of situation cannot be allowed to continue. Openly expressed hostility, especially at meetings, will erode your attempts to build a team for problem solving. You must intercede, starting with a private discussion with each, and then moving to a session with both combatants. They ultimately must agree (both of them) to stop the fighting. Penalty? Transfer or loss of job.

**2. Two of your employees complain about you and your management style**. Here again, you must take action. Have a meeting with each (separately), and see if both have the same complaint, or otherwise. Take their inputs seriously, and explore what you are able to do to make a change. If you honestly conclude that you're okay, but they're not okay, you probably need to move them to a different boss.

**3. One of your employees seems unable to fit in**. He or she can't buy into the "team concept," and wants to get an assignment, and then be left alone. In fact, it's best if the assignment were delivered under the door so as to minimize the direct contact. Here's a case in which you probably need a lot of help from the human resources people. Bring them in to help. A crisis is just around the corner.

Under some circumstances, you can ask two combatants to find a solution, and talk to you when they have done so. As a responsible manager, the best approach is to head off the explosion as best you can. Third (and trusted) parties may be able to give you good advice on how close the explosion is. Take their advice, but keep their confidence.

It's a hard problem, but it cannot really be ignored. Take some steps, and monitor progress very carefully.

# 37

## NEVER MAKE EXCEPTIONS TO THE PROCEDURES IN YOUR POLICY MANUAL, NO MATTER WHAT

Strict adherence to this policy gets you a solid "A" for consistency and rigidity. So if that's what you're looking for, that's likely to be what you'll be getting. And, along with this view will come a reputation for not necessarily caring a whole lot about your people, even though this conclusion may not be fair.

The administrative folks, including your VP for administration, do need some guidelines for handling policy and procedure matters. That part is fine. However, to do their best possible work, they may also need some "elbow-room" in which to exercise their judgment as to what is the best course of action in any given situation. That implies some discretion and some space for interpretation. If the policy and procedures manual takes away all room for judgment, then what's the point of these administrative positions? And who would want to take them?

Having said all that, it is possible to solve this "problem" with an appropriate use of language. For those areas that are likely to require more discretion and flexibility, the following phrases are useful:

▶    at the discretion of, or
▶    under special circumstances, or

▶  when it is in the overall best interest of the company

The last item is actually saying what everyone in the enterprise knows, but usually doesn't think much about. The company executives are free to change any policy and procedure that they do not like, more-or-less at any time. The presumption is that all changes are made "in the best interest of the company." If that presumption turns out to be incorrect, then a deeper problem may exist, leading to a whole lot of difficulties and trouble.

So, what's the bottom line?

Companies need to be flexible and free to exercise judgment about what they do and how they do it. They must look for a path that is beneficial to the company *and* its employees. The administrative folks need to be masters of this process, navigating the ambiguities that arise in just about every enterprise. Flexible language can get you most of the way there. Good will and excellent communications will also help a great deal.

Many items in the policy and procedures manual can be toss-ups in their administration and consequences. One such example is changing from a yearly review to an anniversary date review. Another might be changing the official fiscal year from the government approach to a calendar year system. Other policies affect the individual more than the entire organization, such as paying for two courses per semester instead of one, or paying different amounts, depending upon grades achieved. Erring, if you will, on the side of the employee is not a terrible thing to do—especially when the company has the wherewithal to do so.

# 38

# Don't Employ Management by Objectives (MBO) Practices— They're Old and Outmoded

Management By Objectives (MBO) is indeed "old," as judged by the speed with which "new" wisdom is generated nowadays. MBO is attributed to Peter Drucker, one of the "old time" gurus. Some would say he's the grandfather of all management gurus, and I would agree. Drucker first set forth his MBO ideas in 1954 in his book dealing with the practice of management. Like a fine wine, it has gotten better with age, and usage.

Who are some of the management experts who've followed in Drucker's footsteps? Here's a short list of special advisors and practitioners of the fine art of management:

1. Tom Peters and Robert Waterman
2. Michael Porter
3. Michael Hammer and James Champy
4. Peter Senge
5. Warren Bennis
6. Harold Geneen
7. John P. Kotter
8. William Ouchi
9. Richard Tanner Pascale and Anthony Athos
10. Robert S. Kaplan and David P. Norton
11. David Goleman
12. Jack Welch

Lots of brain power here and lots of good ideas to examine. So can we now conclude that MBO needs to be laid to rest? I don't think so. MBO is still a very powerful and practical idea, with a very strong premise:

> ▶ Set objectives that are agreed to by both manager and employee, and
> ▶ Then try to manage so these objectives are met.

By focusing upon clear discrete objectives, we try to encourage the employee to find his or her own way to approach and solve the problem at hand. We do not micromanage the employee, nor do we insist that the methods used are precisely those that the manager would use. By this means, we encourage independent thinking to satisfy a goal, and leave the pathway to that goal in the hands (and brain) of the employee.

I had the good fortune of operating under an MBO "system" for several years, and I found that it worked well for me in both directions: between me and my boss, and between me and several folks who reported to me. Everyone knew what the objectives were, and readily accepted the concept as fair and sound. And monetary rewards were tied, quantitatively, to meeting the objectives. Subjective judgments were kept to a minimum, and it was not appropriate for new objectives to appear without warning and negotiation. You were able to change the rules at midstream, but all parties had to agree to the new set of rules.

So it does not appear that MBO has become obsolete just because it is "old." It has served us well in the past, and with the appropriate amount of updating and fine tuning, it is likely to be useful as we continue on down the road.

# 39

## DECLINE TO BE A MEMBER OF YOUR BOSS'S TEAM SINCE BUILDING YOUR OWN TEAM IS YOUR FIRST PRIORITY

There are only so many hours in a day and so many days in a week, you reason. Building your own team is your first priority. Since you have always given all your best efforts to your first priority, you're going to do so now. Tough decisions have to be made, and you've never shied away from them. That's what makes you a company asset, and also one of the best managers. You're not here to feather your boss's nest, you reason further. Bosses come and go. But if I build something strong for myself, I will have created a base of strength that will always serve me, at least here. Besides, that's what the company wants.

This line of argument has elements of truth to it—but not enough to lead you to give your boss 0 percent and yourself 100 percent. Not enough to thoroughly reject your boss's possible needs, and not enough to follow a course of action that might well lead you to failure under most sets of circumstances.

So let's look at what you have decided to do from the point of view of your boss. When a boss invites a subordinate to be an active member of his team, it usually means that the boss values the potential contribution you can make. Of course, some bosses will abuse the "membership," and not allow time for anything else. So, in this scenario, the "hidden" feeling might be that your boss does take too much of your time, especially on matters that are not really very important. If that is the case, you are really running from your boss, who does not know how to use you. But keep in mind that as you run, it might be outside the company. Your boss sees that you don't want to be present, and concludes that you are not a "team player." And guess what? He or she may be exactly right.

Let's consider this matter from another angle. An aversion to being part of your boss's team is not a good thing. It usually suggests that something is wrong, either with you or with your boss or both. Under most circumstances, being part of your boss's "inner circle" would carry some satisfaction, and being excluded would do exactly the opposite.

So take another look at your decision and the underlying premises. Maybe you are, in reality, a team buster with respect to your boss. Maybe you have such little respect for your boss that you want to be as far away as possible. Now there's a problem that needs some serious attention.

Yet another scenario is that you may not be flexible enough to work, to your satisfaction, on both your own and your boss's team simultaneously. Maybe you haven't really come to terms with the time that you need to spend building a relationship with your boss. Maximum distance often means minimum relationship, which in turn leads to your getting little or no support from your boss. Few people make it in business without the strong support of the boss (and other people in the firm). Your way of thinking about the problem more or less guarantees that no support will be forthcoming. That's a killer.

# DISREGARD OLD-FASHIONED TOTAL QUALITY MANAGEMENT (TQM) PRINCIPLES

It is true that the rage for Total Quality Management (fondly known as TQM) peaked in the 1980s when many industries used Dr. W. Edwards Deming's theory with its focus on process measurement and controls to make continuous improvement of their products. The automobile and electronics industries come to mind, as if there was a frontal attack on both by the Japanese. It was certainly a perception that they were dealing more effectively with quality matters. It seemed also that new gurus were appearing from all over, explaining their approaches to the problem. You'll probably recognize these names besides Deming's:

1. Philip Crosby
2. Genichi Taguchi
3. Joseph M. Juran
4. Edward Feigenbaum
5. Kaoru Ishikawa

And here are some of the "ideas" developed by the above folks as well as other people:

▶ Deming's 14 Points
▶ Kaizen
▶ Statistical Process Control

- ▶ Quality Circles
- ▶ Pareto Charts
- ▶ Ishikawa Diagrams
- ▶ Quality Function Deployment (QFD)
- ▶ Six Sigma

Despite all the time that has passed since the eighties, we must ask ourselves a basic question: Has the need for high quality products subsided or gone away? The answer has to be an emphatic "No." Indeed, as we continue to recognize global markets, we see that a need for high quality continues to grow. The Japanese are as strong as ever in the delivery of services of high quality (and low price). Now the folks from India are doing the same with their computer-related services.

So the need for high quality remains unabated and the TQM principles remain as relevant as ever with twenty more years to improve the implementation of these principles. That does not make the principles obsolete. Rather, successful implementation serves to reinforce them.

In 2005, I wrote *Managing Complex Systems–Thinking Outside the Box* (John Wiley) that looked at some of the major thrusts from several of our industry leaders. Jack Welch, before he left GE, made sure to re-emphasize the need for quality. Specifically, he established "six sigma" as one (of four) ways to keep GE healthy and growing. Jack Welch continued to support the TQM principles and demonstrate their relevance. And he is just one of a large number of industry leaders to do so.

# Since You're Busy All the Time, Insist Your Direct Reports Make An Appointment If They Wish to See You

There is no doubt that in today's fast moving world all of us are extremely busy—lots of pressures, deadlines, and crises to respond to. Some think that "not enough time in the day" is the culprit, and there's little question that time management *is* critically important. But we need to ask ourselves if "direct report appointments" are the correct way to solve the problem.

After thirty years in industry, at least twenty of which were in some type of management job, I've never really seen this strategy work, and you have to wonder why. The serious manager has concluded that an "open door" policy still remains the best policy. Such an approach means that your direct reports who need to see you can more-or-less walk down the hall and have a high likelihood that your secretary will be able to say "go right in." This doesn't mean you have to stop what you are doing 100 percent of the time. If you are busy and really can't be interrupted, your secretary should be prepared to say, "I'm sorry, she's tied up now, but she'll be able to see you in about 45 minutes." Or something similar. How's that for direct access? A phone call may get even better results. But high levels of access should be the rule rather than the exception.

The "open door policy" has been most successful at Hewlett Packard. In his 1995 book, *The HP Way*, David Packard described their open door policy as "very important at HP because it characterizes the management style to which we are dedicated."[1] That's quite an endorsement.

Solid managers realize that each and every one of their direct reports may well be dealing with urgent issues that need their prompt attention. Requiring appointments sends the wrong signals, isolating the supervisor and creating unnecessary barriers between bosses and employees.

Instead, install an open door policy that acknowledges that the direct report's problem, on any given occasion, may indeed be more important than the manager's problem. Behave as if your folks are dealing with the truly significant matters of the day. Do your part in bashing bureaucracy. Have the "buck stops here" sign on your desk for all to see. Or make up your own sign that conveys that message, like "My time is your time." And this one has music behind it.

[1] David Packard, *The HP Way* (Harper Business, 1995).

# No Hanging Around the Water Cooler—Rigorous Time Management Practices Are Inviolate

## 42

So here we are again, back at "time management." And so soon.

We know we must live and work by rigorous and disciplined time management methods, or get into a lot of trouble. Time is just too precious, and wasting it is sinful. And of all things, once lost, it cannot really be retrieved again.

But is hanging around the coffee room really a waste of time? Taking some time away from your desk and talking with co-workers can be precisely the opposite. In fact, it might be just what you need to clear your head and get a new idea from a colleague. Taking a break may turn out to be exactly what you need to find the answer to a problem whose solution has eluded you.

Some years ago, Peters and Waterman[1] talked about a management practice that is especially relevant to this piece of advice. It was called MBWA, or Management By Walking Around. It was their contention that the apparent lack of rigor and discipline in MBWA was more than offset by its distinct benefits. Digging more deeply into this subject,

---

[1] T. Peters and R. H. Waterman, Jr., *In Search of Excellence* (Warner Books, 1982).

they found that MBWA was actually part of "The HP Way," which David Packard claimed was "coined many years ago by one of our managers,"[2] but actually originated during his days at General Electric. In short, MBWA was a recommended practice for lots of managers. Imagine what you can learn by mingling with the troops. Consider what you might accomplish, just by "walking around," if you are one of the troops.

Remember the advice Professor Harold Hill gave the River City folks in the popular Broadway musical *Music Man* when it was discovered the young folks were playing pool. To get them to stop, he sang, the city had to sponsor a band. Before long, they were all making wonderful music together. Certainly a positive outcome—all resulting from the belief that wasting time is the work of the devil.

Best of all, this positive "waste of time" can be indulged in by both worker and manager as part of what an enterprise values and encourages, rather than a big negative that needs to be stopped. David Packard and his colleague, Bill Hewlett, had it exactly right: People can actually be productive even during breaks if you start trusting them, rather than trying to control what they do around the water cooler.

---

[2] D. Packard, *The HP Way* (Harper Collins, 1995).

# 43

# Don't Share the Company's Plans or Reasons with Your Employees—What They Don't Know Won't Hurt Them

This opens up a variety of interesting, and conflicting, scenarios, like the following.

James, the boss, left for foreign travel with the following good-bye words to George, the loyal employee: "George, please don't forget to give Frank the training we discussed and agreed to—just an hour of each day," whereupon James was out the door, headed for three weeks overseas.

James and George had indeed agreed that George would provide special training for Frank one hour per day on the intricacies and fine points of George's job, just in case. In case what? George was not 100 percent sure, except that it was a good idea and in the best interest of the company, according to James. Not being absolutely clear about the reasons, George started worrying. The company was experiencing some downsizing, so George felt upset and vulnerable. Was he being targeted for replacement? Even the thought made him angry. After all these years of loyal service and superior performance, they might want someone younger and less expensive. Could that be a hidden agenda? And the indignity of it all—to make it easier for the company to let him go by training his own replacement! All this thinking (some call it "catastrophizing") added fuel to George's distress, and probably some points on his blood pressure.

Then George realized that his worry was based on two facts:

▶ James had not given George a good explanation for wanting him to train Frank

▶ George basically did not trust James, or the company.

When there is a lack of information *and* also a lack of trust, it's natural to become suspicious and angry. Of course George would not want to train Frank to take over his own job.

Furthermore, George realized he really didn't like being kept in the dark about his boss's agenda and not being able to trust the company's ultimate goal. So he decided that he would, for the time being, just *not* train Frank, as James wanted. He also made a more fundamental decision. He wanted to be working for a company he trusted and one that respected him enough to tell him, directly, why he was being given each assignment—like giving special training to Frank. He started looking for a new job with a company that had established unambiguous paths for growth, success, and upward mobility, and one that shared information with trust.

# CONTROL MEETINGS BY MAKING SURE YOURS ARE THE ONLY IDEAS PRESENTED AND DISCUSSED

## 44

You've been hounded by your boss to get an important issue resolved. There's lots of pressure on you. Your timeline is short. But you've finally figured out how to solve the problem. NOW it's time for action, and not interminable discussion.

So you call a meeting with your "team," a group of a dozen people, to explain the problem and the reason for time urgency. You go on to articulate the solution you have come up with and your reason to call the meeting—to confirm your solution, and to give out work assignments to each member of the team. These assignments are to implement your solution. You ask if everyone understands his or her assignment, which is to be given first priority. They all say "yes," whereupon you close the meeting.

Is there anything wrong with how you decided to respond to the problem your boss laid on you? The answer is, it's a solution but:

(a) It may be the wrong solution
(b) There may be a clearly better solution
(c) The process you selected has some distinct flaws.

Let's examine this more closely.

Your process clearly does not allow substantive inputs from the members of the team. You've discouraged team problem solving by coming to the table with your solution. You're at the meeting only to make assignments and not to elicit solutions other than your own. This approach subverts the team concept. It also may result in both (a) and (b) above, and either the wrong or a less than best solution.

We cannot guarantee that an approach that asks for ideas for a problem's solution will in fact lead to a better solution. But when you prohibit their suggestions, the message is that your team members can't come up with a better solution. That is distinctly not the way to build a team. That approach, over time, will lead to absenteeism from future meetings, lack of respect, a dysfunctional team, and jumping ship.

It may seem admirable that you are taking active and immediate steps to make a quick decision to solve a real problem. In reality, your actions more or less violate most conventional wisdom about how to create and use a team. Your actions demonstrate a lack of trust and respect for the team members. In reality, your actions give you a distinct push down that slippery slope toward failure. If you want to try a different approach, consider:

▶ Encouraging full participation in problem solving,
▶ Asking a lot of questions, as the leader of the group,
▶ Trying not to leap to any solution too early in the meeting, and
▶ Asking specific members of the team to articulate what they think about the problem and its solution.

Remember, it's not about you. It's about both finding the best solution and also building a team.

# KEEP YOUR DESKTOP CLEAR OF ALL BUT A FEW PAPERS; A CLUTTERED DESK SHOWS A CLUTTERED MIND

This "instruction" may be dead center, but I personally don't understand why.

Over my more than forty-five years in industry and academia, I've seen both types—uncluttered desks and those with the kitchen sink on them. I've always been very impressed with the desk that has only a few papers on it— stacked into vertical piles ready for action. No separators are necessary. Only orderly indentations that appear never to be violated.

I invariably think: "Old Smedley is really organized. Everything has its place. And nothing ever gets lost. And I'll bet that when his boss sees this ultra-superior orderliness, Smedley gets mucho points toward and in favor of his next promotion."

On the other hand, my desk has always been supremely cluttered. How else to find and reach all the papers and sources that need to be at my fingertips? How else to be able to take action without rising from your chair? How else to be truly "into it," other than this immersion in paper? Two distinct work styles. Two ways of interacting with papers and issues. Which is best? Well, it certainly *appears* that a clean desk is the preferred approach. But is this truly the case?

Let's get some help from a third party. I decided to look around for ideas on this issue from an authoritative source. I had a copy of Geneen's book[1] on my bookshelf so I retrieved it (rather easily, I might add; it was on the shelf alphabetically). I went to the index and immediately found "clean-desk executive, pp. 157-69". Upon further examination, I found twelve pages—all of chapter 7—called "The Cluttered Desk Executive." I started to read, expecting Geneen to really blast such an executive. Well, the opposite turned out to be the case. Here are some things ITT's guru had to say:

▶ When I find a "gleaming empty, clean desk top, I am dealing with a fellow who is so far removed from the realities of his business that someone else is running it for him."

▶ "You want to grab the information you need at the moment. It has to be on your desk"

▶ "My desk was cluttered because I immersed myself in the company's ongoing business."

Well, it certainly was clear where Geneen stood. I was just about as pleased as I could be. We had similar "desktop" habits, though his was a more extreme case of organized clutter. Vindication is wonderful, but one day I'm going to find a guru who argues just the reverse. I will not be happy when that happens.

[1] H. Geneen, with A. Moscow, *Managing* (Avon Books, 1984).

# LOOK AS IF YOU ARE LISTENING BUT BE READY WITH YOUR NEXT VERBAL ASSAULT

You reached your current position, in part, by mastering the fine art of creating impressions. You clearly know the difference between impression and reality, and have decided to put more time in on the impression side. Not a bad strategy, except for the possible dangers of totally losing sight of reality—especially if your impressionism includes pretending to listen to people who are trying to communicate with you.

You start out with intense eye-to-eye contact that remains unswerving during the interaction. This is supported by positive shakes of the head when it seems appropriate to do so. "Message received, and I agree with what you're saying." Pretty powerful stuff. A more sophisticated response is to lift your eyebrows and wrinkle your brow, again, as appropriate. A small dose of all this, and the speaker is just about convinced that you are the best and most concerned listener they've ever spoken to. They also believe that you agree with what they've been saying (the power of impressions). Never had a boss or colleague so good at listening.

The reality (what is that?). You're mulling over a host of matters not at all related to what the speaker is trying to convey to you. After all, you need your own time to solve your own problems. Why not use the time when someone is talking to you, if you know how to do so. You do this by being able to multi-process in this very peculiar way: Stay at the edge of listening while, at the same time, make progress with the problems that have been plaguing you.

Another rather powerful variant is to appear to be listening, but in reality (that word again) you are preparing a rebuttal point. This approach is particularly strong if you're talking to an adversary or an opponent. Rebuttal points often begin with:

> ▶  "I agree with that, but . . ."
> ▶  "I cannot completely agree because of the fact that . . ."
> ▶  "I hear you, but I have some concerns about . . ."
> ▶  "Your position is interesting, but does it actually solve . . .?"

You've mastered the fine art of appearing to be fully engaged, when in fact you are only half present. Your agenda is ultimately to get your point across, rather than truly understand what is being said to you. Without that understanding, current and future conversations are likely to be superficial. That will be the reality (that word again). The impression will be quite different, depending upon how good you are at faking it.

Is this the way you want to lead your life?

Is this the new formula for how to succeed in business?

You may also be missing some really good ideas.

# GET YOUR DIRECT REPORTS TO COMPETE FURIOUSLY AGAINST EACH ANOTHER

If you buy this suggestion, you have many ways to move forward. Let's explore some of them.

An important aspect of implementing this strategy is to hold lots of meetings, as well as one-on-one get-togethers. At the meetings, you want to ask a lot of questions so that your direct reports can have a chance to express their ideas in front of you, as well as their colleagues. Instead of just accepting these ideas, you can make a point by taking an "evaluative" stance most of the time, like labeling the ideas "good," or "not fully thought through," and all manner of other shades of evaluation. The message will be received without your saying so directly. You're constantly judging them. You're keeping score in your head, and that score will have a lot to do with pay, promotion, and prestige. Isn't the business world wonderful?

The reactions of your people can basically take one of two directions, and each is likely to be an individual choice. If they "buy" what you are doing, they will start to compete with one another, looking for positive evaluations from you. If such is the case, your power is increasing and your people are in search of your overt approval. However, not everyone will buy your approach. These people will begin to voice their objections with you in private. They'll know it's too risky to challenge you in an open meeting. But you hold most of the cards, including the opportunity to question their ability to compete, to run away from competitive situations, and the like. We can only express remorse for those who take you on in this situation.

Now, let's ask the question: Why would you accept this way of managing your people? Is it because you believe that internal competition will lead to better performance? And better performance will lead to higher individual productivity. It will also allow you to "see" how your people react to lots of pressure and a competitive environment. You believe that the "fittest will survive" and have a better chance at being promoted and moving the company forward. This, in turn, will reflect itself in a positive profile for the price of the stock. You believe that you are helping your people mature and face the realities of the world they're in. Face reality. That's what GE's Jack Welch emphasized.[1]

Now, at this point, try to take a contrarian position. Is there any value in stressing cooperation instead of competition? Is your intuition telling you that the cooperative approach will be more beneficial to everyone, including you, the boss? Does the competitive approach feel highly manipulative, and even dishonest, at some level? Pick up a few books on teambuilding and read them thoroughly before you come to a definite answer. Which approach is more likely to lead you to success? Which approach has a significant chance of putting you on that downward path? If you can't decide, find a season's collection of "The Apprentice" videos that will reveal new and advanced forms of internecine warfare.

[1] J. Welch with J. Byrne, *Jack – Straight From the Gut* (Warner Books, 2001).

# Reprimand Your People at Meetings So Everyone Can Learn From Their Mistakes

You might well think that public humiliation is a learning experience, but not everyone appreciates being humiliated in front of their colleagues. They'll live in dread of each meeting as a time of punishment, rather than creative problem solving.

If you are into humiliation, you'd better do it quickly, since most people so treated will be off to another company as soon as they can find another job.

You've got to question the premise that people can learn something constructive from being reprimanded in front of others. For most people, getting beaten up in public is not conducive to learning, except to inspire the natural instinct to depart, or fight back, and as soon as possible.

Now there may be situations where one or more of your people have made egregious mistakes. You, as boss, are furious about these errors. So you lose your cool and convey your anger in no uncertain terms:

- ▶ "How could you have done such a stupid thing?"
- ▶ "We role-played that scenario, and you failed miserably in this real world situation."
- ▶ "You were supposed to talk to me before you did a handshake with that customer."

- ▶ "You teamed with exactly the wrong company. Now we've got twice as much work to do."
- ▶ "Your price was clearly too low. Now we lose $250 for every widget we sell, and we have an army out there selling widgets!"

There *are* ways to discuss errors, but a reprimand is hardly a good way to begin. However, it is certainly legitimate to figure out how to convey lessons learned from mistakes. Try this:

> I'm not pleased with what we did in negotiating a contract with the XYZ corporation. Having just examined the terms of that contract, I'd like to hear your reactions. John, please, can you start the discussion. What do you think? Can you cite some pluses and minuses? Then we'll go around the room and continue to discuss.

Here you're making clear that an error was made, but you're also trying to be constructive and understand all aspects of the situation. You've thrown the ball to your people in a non-threatening way. In that environment, they're likely to be listening, thinking, and learning. Finish by constructing on the whiteboard all the pluses and minuses, with notes on how to handle such a situation should it, or something like it, arise again.

# NEVER REENGINEER YOUR BUSINESS PROCESSES IN HOUSE— FARM IT OUT TO THE PROS

Let's start with the assumption that you are considering some set of Business Process Reengineering (BPR) activities because you realize that one or more of the business processes under your control are broken or in need of some serious overhaul. Michael Hammer and James Champy, the originators of BPR,[1] said basically if you don't like the results you're getting in a particular business area, change the process(es) that led to these unsatisfactory results. Sounds easy, but Hammer and Champy told us it wasn't.

For instance, you may be unhappy with the length of time it takes to:

- ▶ Produce about half of your products
- ▶ Review and turn around your contracts
- ▶ Service your customers with warrantees
- ▶ Send out invoices
- ▶ Produce project cost reports
- ▶ Make simple decisions.

---

[1] M. Hammer and J. Champy, *Reengineering the Corporation* (HarperBusiness, 1993).

If you dig a bit deeper, you can find another dozen or so areas in need of a serious dose of BPR. However, it is how to go about reengineering these processes that needs to be addressed. One way is to "farm out" the BPR tasks to a professional services company that specializes in this type of reengineering. They're the pros, they know how to do it, and therefore they will do a good job. Many companies have taken this approach—an entire BPR consulting industry has grown out of it. However, before farming out the work, consider these three factors:

1.    BPR consultants are very expensive.
2.    Success rates have hovered around 33-1/3 percent (two-thirds of BPR consultancy efforts have not been successes).
3.    A simple alternative that is more cost-effective is to find a dedicated and capable person in your company who can lead the charge toward an *internal* grassroots BPR activity. The premise here is that people within the company are mostly ready, willing, and able to define and then make the necessary process changes—if properly led and motivated. And they won't have to spend months learning what the current processes are, they already know them. As for making productive changes, they know how to do that too.

A friend of mine, also the president of a local company, called me to explore his need for BPR. We decided to try the internal approach, with me serving as facilitator. The results were excellent, and the costs were extremely low, as compared to bringing in a consulting company. My friend was more than pleased, and I was convinced of the efficacy of this approach. Real solutions from internal people? Try it; you'll like it.

## MAKE DECISIONS QUICKLY TO MAINTAIN FORWARD MOMENTUM AND RESPECT

This one is very close to the edge. Knowing when and how to make decisions is a deep and complicated subject. Hundreds of explorers of the fine art of decision-making have given us the benefit of their thinking and experimentation. Here are but two areas of this subject that stand out.

The first is that decision-making is highly situation-dependent. Put the same person into two different situations and the time for making decisions could be very different, even though the "style" is the same. The second is a small bias in the direction of action as opposed to "paralysis by analysis." MBA graduates are taught how to analyze a situation from top to bottom. Practitioners tend to feel more urgency to act, where such action leads to progress and closure.

Along these lines, we get a very useful perspective by going back to Peters' and Waterman's classic study of the eight attributes of excellence.[1] One of these is a "Bias For Action," closely aligned with a tendency to make rapid decisions.

Rapid decision-making moves us on down the road, to be sure. But "maintaining momentum" is probably not

[1] T. Peters & R. Waterman, Jr., *In Search of Excellence* (Harper & Row, 1982).

the most important benefit. It's not like you're trying to win a race or keep from falling asleep on the job. Which raises the most interesting and relevant question: What exactly are you trying to do? A reasonable answer to that might be: You're trying to make the right decision in a timely manner. The emphasis here is on the word "right." A wrong decision usually doesn't get us too far (though it might get us nowhere quickly).

And while we're on the matter of "right" let's look at what Peter Drucker said about that important five letter word: "A good leader does the right things; a good manager does things right."[2]

So what then is the bottom line? For this author, it has to tilt in the direction of correctness instead of speed. From time to time, speed can indeed be crucial. But ultimately we must favor the manager who knows how to make the right decision, even if it is not done quickly. If the passage of time invalidates the decision, then we must say the decision was, in fact, wrong. It was an implicit choice that did not recognize time as one of the key decision factors.

On the matter of respect for rapid decision-making, that respect is usually tempered by the ultimate result. If you make a quick decision, you often get a few positive points for decisiveness. If you make what turns out to be the wrong decision, all semblance of respect will be gone, in just about an instant. So take a little more time, and try to make sure that your course of action is well chosen, and correct.

[2] H. Eisner, *Reengineering Yourself & Your Company* (Artech House, 2000).

# PROTECT YOUR AUTHORITY AND POSITION AS BOSS BY NEVER VEERING FROM YOUR OWN WELL-THOUGHT-OUT SOLUTIONS

Consider this scenario.

It is no accident that you have become the boss. You've labored very hard to get where you are, working all kinds of extra hours, over many years. Add to that the fact that you've got an MBA from a high-ranking Ivy League School, from which you graduated in the top five percent of the class. So you've got all the right credentials and you're on the right track in your company. Just keep doing what you've been doing.

A serious strength in your method of operation is to call meetings of your teams (you have several) that require massive amounts of personal preparation. You define and analyze each issue in great detail because it reminds you of the case study work you did in graduate school. You looked at every factor and every variable to examine causes, effects, and how they might contribute to defining the right course of action. You invariably got an A or an A plus for this outstanding work, which was a source of delight to you. And you used these same methods in all your work assignments, including the current ones.

So when you call a meeting to order, you are able to

distribute an agenda where you've studied and analyzed each item, defined the problems, and set forth your solutions. In fact, even if the agenda is only three items long, you've chewed on each for at least several hours—like another case study come alive in the real world. This time, however, you have complete control over what issues are addressed and what solutions are brought to bear. The transfer from academia to industry, for you, has been seamless and you know how better than anyone.

So, at your meeting, you define the problems and set forth your solutions. Your agenda is a tour de force—and you know it. And so do the members of your teams. Having read about team building, you ask your people for reactions to your presentations.

Uh oh, a few people are daring to suggest an approach different from yours. Of course you have already considered and rejected this approach for various reasons. And now, here's a suggestion that may even be as good as yours, but you do not want to be viewed as weak or not well prepared, so you reject this idea as well. After all, you usually do have the best answers and solutions, when all was said and done. How could it be otherwise, with your prodigious education and work ethic? They paid off in school, and they're continuing to pay off in the complex world of industry.

Lately, you've noticed that your teams have been losing some of your best people. They either asked for transfers or got a job in another company. They may never find a mentor and problem solver as good as you. Well, that's their loss. Any questions?

# CELEBRATING COMPANY SUCCESSES IS A WASTE OF MONEY AND TIME THAT COULD BE PUT TO MORE PRODUCTIVE USE

## 52

The only thing worse than not celebrating your successes is not having any successes to celebrate.

Some managers take the position that true (and elaborate) celebrations of success are absolutely a waste of time and money. Perhaps they think it will lead to a period of low productivity, or that the same time and money can be put to better uses. Or possibly they saw their favorite team lose the seventh game of the World Series and have hated boisterous celebrations of success since then (especially the wasting of perfectly good champagne).

Over the years, I have found celebrations very useful and appropriate, assuming they are not overdone. When they are tastefully expressed, they can be strong motivators and ways to bring team members closer to one another. Sharing good times is not to be underestimated and can have several consequences. One is that it shows respect for a winning effort and a winning team. Success tends to breed success, and people want to be part of it. The feeling is contagious; the acknowledgment is reinforcing.

Second, successful efforts and teams are models for behavior that can be emulated by others. This generally means that other folks in the enterprise should be informed about the celebrations, as well as the ingredients that went into the success.

Third, celebrations can be opportunities to capture "lessons learned." Why, for instance, was the team successful? What did they do to assure their success? What kind of competition did they have to contend with? How important was (a) the work plan, (b) company experience and reputation, (c) the assigned team, (d) the proposed schedule, and (e) the proposed budget. Were there any special (unique) approaches that were employed (e.g., best-value contracting, indirect cost reductions, etc.)?

Company management can see celebrations as special opportunities to acknowledge the kinds of behavior that it desires and wishes to support—all across the enterprise. If the success is "big enough," it can be accompanied by special rewards such as bonuses.

Taking off from Gertrude Stein, a success is a success is a success. They can be few and far between. They can be years in the making. They can be, for some people, once in a lifetime events. Don't we all deserve a celebration when we've done something out of the ordinary? Or would we rather focus our attention on how to fail?

# BACKWORD

Well, you've now been through all 52 prescriptions for retrograde motion in your company. I don't know if the journey has been rapid (i.e., a week or so) or slow (like 52 weeks); but I hope it has been enjoyable and engaging. The least your efforts should repay to you are several hours of provocative thoughts—of all shapes and sizes. See if any of these half dozen reactions ring true to you:

- ▶ "No sensible boss would ever do that."
- ▶ "Upon reflection, I really can't agree with that point of view."
- ▶ "That does make sense, and I will share it with the folks at work tomorrow to see what they think."
- ▶ "What good are negatives? I want the positives."
- ▶ I think I'll crunch through this book again to see what has stuck and what hasn't."
- ▶ Yes, of course, this is the perfect gift for my boss —with a message from me on the inside cover."

Looking back at the "Midword," I feel compelled to convey to you (and myself) another "Top Ten," drawn from the last 26 items (27 through 52). They are numbers 30, 33, 34, 37, 38, 40, 44, 45, 50, and 52. No further comment on these appears necessary. But I do want to say that there are a few things I've learned from writing this book.

The first is that if I ever sit down to write a companion book, with another 52 suggestions, I don't believe I'll have much difficulty finding yet another 52 ideas on which to focus. It would seem that the number of ways to fail, while not infinite, is more than I would care to try to estimate. I doubt the well will run dry.

The second is my amazement at the good sense that is already documented somewhere within the numerous books in my own personal library. Of course, I love to buy books, especially about business. Some day, do a "Google" on "Peter Drucker" or on the key words "teamwork" or "team building." Simply astonishing.

And finally, my third lesson learned is that there's much old wisdom that gets re-cast all the time, in a relentless process of renewal. The mind is wonderfully inventive, seeking and conveying new results and perspectives from both old and new data. And just watching companies "do their thing" provides all the information we need. The "laboratories" are out there, producing new data all the time from what they are doing, and what they are not doing— day by day, even 24 by 7. Keep your eye on them. It's a lot of fun.

# LAST WORD

As the author of this diminutive treatise, I wish to thank you as well as commend you for reaching this "Last Word." I have tried to convey several messages about how to fail and, of course, how not to fail. As you know, they are (almost) flip sides of one another. Avoiding failure pathways certainly can help us find choices that will ultimately lead to success.

Having discussed some 52 ways to fail, I am hopeful that some of these might make a positive contribution in your life. You have noticed, I'm sure, that several of my "suggestions" are close to the edge. That is, with the appropriate care and attention you can find pluses and minuses, depending upon degree and situation. For clarity's sake, I've tried to explore when you might actually be stepping over an edge. Perhaps, in the final analysis, there are not that many "absolutes." After all, there once was a time when management by command authority was considered the right way to go. Indeed, if you wear a uniform, it is still considered the proper way to manage a large complicated organization. But what is appropriate for a military person is not necessarily the right answer for a modern industrial organization manager.

Several of my footnotes are intended to steer you to a handful of books that, over the years, I have found to be especially useful. The "bonuses" to this book, if you will, are the several books that I have cited that tell critical parts of the management story. And now that I am looking back, I can see that I have left out more than I have included. Perhaps that is a small signal to me to think about a next book of seriously important topics. "Teamwork" is one such area that remains a centerpiece of powerful and progressive management. There are many others.

Despite all that has been written, and from a variety of angles, there still appear to be large numbers of folks who believe their bosses are complete disasters—sometimes as managers, sometimes also as human beings. Someday we'll find out if this "number" is more like 30 or more like 70 percent. If it turns out to be something like the latter, it will be a good news/bad news story. The bad news is that we're messing up rather extensively. The good news is that (a) there's lots of room for improvement, and (b) our lack of competence hasn't (apparently) brought us to our knees. Of course, the "game" isn't over yet. Several books and articles claim that we are already trying to move forward from a kneeling position.

So as I close, I'm reminded of the time when several of my colleagues and I were working as a subcontractor to a large company. We proposed a new and somewhat progressive idea, which was listened to intently by their chief engineer. Then he said, "Sounds good, but I can't give you an answer right now. I'm going to have to confer with my Manglement about this." Yes, often there's "Manglement" to keep in the loop and contend with.